THE RIDDLE
OF THE WINDS

THE RIDDLE
OF THE WINDS

W. S. Kals

Illustrated by the author

5058 H. S.
DOUBLEDAY & COMPANY, INC.
GARDEN CITY, NEW YORK
1977

ISBN: 0-385-01231-4
Library of Congress Catalog Card Number: 76-2785
Copyright © 1977 by William S. Kals
ALL RIGHTS RESERVED
PRINTED IN THE UNITED STATES OF AMERICA
FIRST EDITION

FOR
KAREN,
MARIA,
AND
JANE

Contents

Some Puzzling Questions

What causes the wind? What makes the wind blow now from one direction, now from another? What makes winds gentle or savage, wet or dry, warm or cold?

What would earth be like without winds? What's the wind's contribution in shaping the land? What its role in the lives of plants, animals, men, and nations?

How can a winter wind after crossing snow-covered mountains bring springlike warmth? How can a nor'easter move in from the southwest?

Are the trade winds of the tropics and subtropics the exhalation of sargassum weed? If not, what causes these most regular of all winds?

What are the jet streams, which were only discovered in the 1940s? How do these high-altitude winds affect you and me, day in and day out?

What's the true connection between high and low barometric pressure and wind? How can you read wind direction from a weather map that doesn't show winds?

We know what drives the wind machine of tropical storms; but why aren't there more hurricanes and typhoons? Why none in the South Atlantic? And why do the experts still argue about the mechanism responsible for tornadoes and waterspouts?

Can a spinning dishpan serve as a model of the winds in the northern or southern hemisphere? Can a computer, starting from a windless condition, trace the wind systems of the entire world?

And what about using the energy of the wind? Will wind-generated power soon compete with fossil fuels, even nuclear energy?

W.S.K.

THE RIDDLE
OF THE WINDS

1

Wind—Early Explanations

This is a book about wind. So you'll expect me to explain what causes the winds. Everywhere, from the earliest times, people have speculated about that.

Rather than have me bore you with a long list of beliefs from many places and different times, let me just present my personal favorite among them: the tree theory. Trees cause the wind. You can check that easily yourself. When the leaves are motionless, there's no wind. When the leaves begin to rustle, you'll notice a slight breeze; when small branches move, you'll feel a moderate breeze. Whole trees in motion give you a gale.

You may object: "What causes the wind on a prairie with not a tree in sight?" That's easily answered: "Trees beyond the horizon."

You must not object that the tree theory seems to mix up cause and effect. The two seem inseparable in weather science. Does the wind bring the weather, or does a passing weather system bring certain winds? As you will see, cause and effect are still intertwined in the most sophisticated explanation of winds. Wind in the northern hemisphere blows so that high pressure is to its right. But also, a steady wind *creates* high pressure on its right in the northern hemisphere.

Perhaps I have gone too fast. Perhaps I should have started by defining wind. A bright child will tell you, "It's moving air." If you ask the right questions, you can sharpen the definition. "Is the cold air that seeps in around the window wind?" "No, that's a draft." "The air moving out of a panting dog's mouth, is that wind?" "No, that's not enough air."

"So we agree, it must be a large quantity of air moving," a Socrates might sum it up. But he wouldn't leave it there. "Does air in wind move mostly up, down, or sideways?" Most people will agree that what they call wind usually blows sideways, roughly along the ground.

You may object that *air*—stuff we normally don't see, taste, or smell—was too abstract a concept for primitive man. I think you are swaying the wrong tree. The great abstraction is in the word wind. Steady breezes and gusty gales, gentle airs that fan your skin, storms that lash it, blown dust that sandpapers it, blizzards that needle it . . . to call all these and others "winds" requires sophistication.

But how to explain these different winds? You can create a miniature wind, say when you blow into a beginning campfire. Why then should a god not be able to make a full-scale wind? That theory is so reasonable that we find it with variations among many ancient or primitive cultures. Usually there is one god—or giant, or spirit—for each wind. The spirits take turns in blowing at you; sometimes they all take a night or even a day off, and you get a calm.

And what to call these different winds? You could suit yourself: Name the wind after a god, giant, or spirit; or name it after the area where he lives and blows.

Years ago I came across a list of several hundred names of winds in different parts of the world. Some had poetic names: Eliseos, Solano, Papagayos. . . . At least they sounded poetic. Translated they may just have meant "the bloody awful one."
I added names to that list whenever I came across some local wind name. But at least one wind god didn't like my collection. He sent a freak blast that wrecked my little ship, and the list was lost.

No great loss for you, really. Many of the names referred to the same wind in different languages. Worse, the same name described a fierce, parching wind in Africa and a gentle, moist breeze in Italy.

Naming local winds made praying for them, or complaining about them, convenient. But philosophically the one-god-one-wind explanation didn't satisfy the ancient Greeks. They came up with a unified wind theory. A single god, Aeolus, was in charge of all winds. He kept them locked in a cave with eight—or twelve—openings, each normally blocked by a big rock. According to mood, he'd roll away one or another of these rocks. Just a crack for a breeze; halfway for a moderate gale; all the way for a storm.

If you don't believe that could work, you probably won't believe either that he gave Ulysses a wineskin full of wind to be released whenever he needed it.

The Babylonians tried to link the winds—and everything else—to the motion of the heavenly bodies. In a given place, when the sun is in the sign of Cancer you'll have warm weather and southerly winds; when it's in Capricorn you'll have cold weather and northerly winds. Translation: It is warm in summer, cold in winter; here southerly winds prevail in summer, northerly winds in winter.

To improve this explanation, or forecast, they tried to link the shifting winds with the motions of Mercury, Venus, Mars, Jupiter, and Saturn. The results were disappointing; the planets just don't move fast enough to account for the frequent wind changes.

But then there was the moon, easily observed and changing shape dramatically in monthly cycles. It rises and sets, on an average, almost an hour later each succeeding day and races through the zodiac at the rate of one sign in little more than two days.

That's plenty of action, easily observed. Perhaps that is the reason why all over the world people who have never heard of the Babylonians, and without knowledge of astrology, have rules that relate wind and weather to the moon. Some rules relate to the phases of the moon; others to its rising and setting; yet others to the highest position of the moon in the sky, the moon's southing.

For a more scientific early explanation of the winds you might start by looking in the wide-ranging writings of Aristotle (384–322 B.C.). Some scholars think these writings were lecture notes, preparation for courses he gave at his school, the Lyceum in Athens. Perhaps they are expanded notes of lectures he had already given. What lecturer has never regretted having talked to so few listeners?

You'll probably think you have found what you were looking

for—an explanation of the winds—when you come across a work titled *Meteorologica*. But Aristotle includes many phenomena outside what we call meteorology, the science of weather. He deals, for instance, with shooting stars, still called meteors. (We now know them to be bits of matter that burn when they enter the atmosphere; larger pieces that survive the trip and reach the ground are now called meteorites.)

Aristotle also discusses in that work comets, earthquakes, and the Milky Way. (Now anyone with binoculars can see that the Milky Way is a concentration of many stars; in the days of naked-eye observation it was a mystery.)

Rain, sleet, dew, snow, hail, and hoarfrost—all of which Aristotle also discusses—are still officially called *hydrometeors*, that is, atmospheric water vapor in any form.

Given the title of the work, you may give Aristotle credit for having invented the term meteorology. Not so. In the very first paragraph he refers to "what all our predecessors have called meteorology."

You may have heard these predecessors—e.g., Anaximander, Anaximenes, Democritus, Empedocles, and Heraclitus—referred to as pre-Socratic philosophers. Socrates himself had died fifteen years before Aristotle was born. But Socrates' star pupil, Plato, was Aristotle's teacher for twenty years.

Aristotle's meteorology, in the sense of weather science, contains some keen observations and shrewd conclusions. He explains, for example, the water cycle. "All precipitation runs down rivers or seeps through the ground to marshes, lakes, and the sea. In these places it evaporates to start the cycle all over."

But observation and conclusions was not his method in *Meteorologica*. Instead he set himself an impossibly difficult task: He was going to explain all the phenomena by pure logic.

ONE: He required every statement to be self-evident or to be logically derived from self-evident statements.

(That works—more or less—in geometry, as Euclid soon tried to prove. But it can lead you astray in the natural sciences. In *Meteorologica* we learn, for example, that hot water freezes quicker than cold water. That's why, the author tells us in an aside, ice fishermen in Pontus use *hot* water to repair cracks in the ice. Had rising "steam" misled him into thinking the water must have been hot? Or were the fishermen pouring hot water on the ice to make a *hole*—or enlarge one? It was centuries before anyone took two buckets—one filled with cold, one with hot water—outside in winter and reported which froze first.)

TWO: Aristotle's orderly mind made him limit his "principles" to a minimum. He chose four: fire, air, water, and earth. Translate that as four principles, four bodies, or four elements. Then add: "Fire occupies the highest places, earth the lowest. Between them air is nearest to fire, water to earth."

THREE: All motion must be simple. It can be circular, or directly toward the center of earth (call it straight down), or away from the center (straight up).

In this framework Aristotle had his work—including explaining wind and weather—cut out for himself. He candidly confesses, "Some of the phenomena admit explanation; others still puzzle us."

As he proceeds, he often violates his first rule and argues, in the best Greek tradition, by analogy. Example: "There are those who maintain that all winds are the same. That's as absurd as to say that all rivers are one river."

Some of his statements about weather phenomena read as if he had copied them from a text to be written more than two thousand years later. "Clouds don't usually form near the ground because the air is heated by radiation reflected by the earth. Clouds do form where the warming rays reflected by the earth diminish. Then why don't clouds form in the uppermost atmosphere? Because it's warm and dry." It is, but it took balloons and rockets and instruments to find that out.

He states that dew, drizzle, rain, snow, and hoarfrost are the same thing. And that small droplets by uniting form larger drops, which fall as, say, rain. Quite so.

But don't think Aristotle could pick the brains of meteorologists yet unborn. His correct statements are supported by some very questionable arguments. Example: All heat on earth comes from the sun. Correct. Now the explanation: To give heat, a motion must be both rapid and near. The motion of the stars is rapid, but distant; the moon's is near but slow. Only the sun's motion is fast enough and near enough to warm the earth.

You are interested in winds. What has he got to say about them?

He starts the chapter with a complaint. "No theory has been handed down to us that the most ordinary man could not have thought of. Some say that air in motion is wind, that the same air when it condenses becomes clouds and rain. Some of my predecessors maintained that the winds appeared to differ depending on the region from which they happen to blow."

The predecessors were about right. But Aristotle has another explanation: There are two kinds of emanations, both caused by the sun. One is water vapor, which is moist and cold; the other, for which there is no accepted name, is smokelike, warm, and dry. (Call it *dry exhalation*, if you like.) One can not exist without the other. When we speak of one, we mean it predominates. Sunshine raises moist exhalation. When the sun is weak or hidden, the cold makes the water vapor condense back into water which falls to earth.

That, according to Aristotle, is the reason why in winter—when the sun is weak—and at night it rains more than in summer and in daytime.

For those who might object that it doesn't rain more at night he adds: "At night people are likely not to notice the rain." (The physicist's approach, measuring the rainfall by day and by night for at least a year, was not his style.)

Now comes his crucial point: "The dry emanation is the source and substance of all winds."

"Dry air and water vapor appear in their proper mixture according to the seasons. Now there is an excess of vapor, now of dry emanation." The changing proportions also explain why some years are cold and wet, others windy and dry. Each of the two exhalations goes into neighboring districts *separately*. That explains why one district may have floods, while a nearby one has a drought.

But what causes the exhalations—dry or wet—to move? At one point, faithful to his restriction to simple motions, he gives credit to the revolution of the heavens. What we now would call the *apparent* revolution, or simply the rotation of earth itself. (We shall see later that this rotation influences, but does not cause winds.) But how does the revolution of the heavens make the two exhalations travel in different paths and at different speeds? Aristotle does not say.

Rotation of sky or earth can explain an east wind, as we shall see in an early theory on trade winds. But what about a north and a south wind, which Aristotle calls the most frequent winds? He explains them by the sun's seasonal travel across the equator.

He gives a wind rose of twelve directions and names the ten winds most common in Athens. He observed that when one wind ceases it is replaced in an orderly way by one clockwise nearest on the wind rose. (This shifting "with the sun," e.g., from northeast to east to southeast, which we call veering—as opposed to a counterclockwise shift, against the sun, called backing—is the usual shift not just in Athens but generally in the northern hemisphere.)

He states that winds out of opposite directions are impossible, but that two winds from nearby directions, say northeast and southeast, can blow at the same time. He does not mean the wind direction may vary from minute to minute and keep a wind vane busy, but that two sailing vessels may arrive at a port at the same time, one having been pushed by a wind from the northeast, one by a wind from the southeast.

How does Aristotle explain windless periods, calms? "The dry exhalations are quenched either by frost or excessive heat." Calms also occur when it's neither very cold nor very hot. Explanation: The dry exhalations either have not yet had time to form or have blown away to other parts.

Earthquakes, according to Aristotle, are caused by wind rushing into the earth. That's why you'll notice a calm during most earthquakes. But if you do feel a wind, that's not the one that caused the quake but a second wind.

It is unfortunate that *Meteorologica* became the source of knowledge about winds—and much else—for the next two thousand years.

The treatise *De Ventis* (on winds) by Theophrastus, Aristotle's longtime student and hand-picked successor as head of the Lyceum, would have been better.

Theophrastus set himself a simpler task than Aristotle. He didn't try to explain comets, earthquakes, and other phenomena by the same mechanism that explains winds. And he saw nothing wrong in describing the winds at a given season at a certain place without proving from first principles that such winds had to blow and no others. He did not try to tie the winds to the circular motion of the heaven. He saw that Aristotle's concept of dry exhalations led to more problems than it solved. Out of respect for the master he didn't refute that theory; he dropped it quietly.

In Athens, as near many coasts, breezes toward the sea alternate with breezes from the sea. Sometimes these breezes, changing in a regular daily pattern, are the only winds felt. At other times they strengthen or weaken already existing winds. If wind is *dry* exhalation, it can not form over water. A sea breeze is impossible. Aristotle tried to explain the impossible as a rebound of wind from some offshore island. Theophrastus's explanation: The cool of night, followed by the rising of the sun, followed again by night. That accounts for the direction *and* the timing of these winds.

The sun and the heat content of the air in Theophrastus's treatise act as the mover not only of these winds but of all others also.

He returns to the simple definition of all winds: air in motion. Winds are dry or moist, hot or cold, depending on the region from which they come. That, as we have seen, was not a new thought.

But Theophrastus went one step farther. The character of the wind is changed by the lands or seas over which it has come. He doesn't state that as a general principle—which it is—but in examples. For instance, the south wind in North Africa is dry, but passing over the Mediterranean it becomes more prone to bring rain the farther north it moves.

Theophrastus recognized another modifier of the wind: the landscape, an important factor in mountainous Greece. He observed the strengthening of a wind moving through a pass and compares it to the rush of a placid river when hemmed in by a narrow gorge. He also observed that rain falls when the wind drives clouds against a mountain.

I don't want to leave the impression that a slight revision of Theophrastus's treatise could serve as a text of modern wind theory. There are many pieces of the puzzle still missing. Example: He could not explain why winds seemingly from cold regions blew warmly down mountain slopes.

Three generations of teachers—Socrates, Plato, and Aristotle—led him into many traps of apparently flawless reasoning. But his work on winds could have prompted other people to observe local winds and explain them.

Instead they read *Meteorologica*.

2

Winds and the Land, Plants, and Animals

Without winds our world would be a very different place.

Even the maps would be somewhat different. True, the continental plates and their slow movement over the surface of our globe have nothing to do with the winds. And mountains are built by faulting, or by folding after two such plates have collided. Example: the Himalayas as a result of the bumping of the Indian plate into the one that carries Europe and most of Asia. Mountains are also built by volcanoes, which again have nothing to do with winds.

It is also true that mountains are worn away mostly by water. Sometimes the water is frozen into glaciers, small and local, or—during ice ages—on a continental scale. And water in a small crack wedges a rock apart as it expands on freezing.

The wind helps a little in the process of erosion. You'll see the result in the smooth wind-sculpted rocks of arid regions, such as the Needles in Utah.

You'll see the result also at the base of telephone poles after a sandstorm. Near the ground, where the wind carries the largest grains of sand, the pole is chewed away as if a beaver had been at work.

If you ever get caught in a dust storm in your car as I was once in Nevada, you'll see the action on your automobile. It'll be sandblasted right down to bare metal on the windward side, and your windshield will be turned into frosted glass.

But the wind also thwarts the eroding work of water. It saves the fine material that streams and glaciers have stockpiled for later disposal at sea. The wind blows the material away from the stream bed and redistributes it over the land. This *loess*—sometimes hundreds of feet deep—forms some of the most fertile lands in the world. Examples are to be found in the Mississippi drainage basin, Argentina, and China.

Onshore winds on sandy beaches snatch material from the very edge of the sea and form low dunes. Waves bring in more sand to make up the loss, and the process of dune building continues. Meanwhile the wind blows off the top of the dune and that material settles farther inland. More sand is brought in by the wind to replace the lost dune top. As more of that is blown off, a second dune builds up downwind. And that process continues until rows of dunes seem to march inland. You can see that process in action on the east coast of the United States from Cape Cod south, wherever plants or man have not stopped the march.

All of Florida was put on the map by such dunes, helped by sand-trapping mangroves, and—in some places—by the shelter of coral reefs against erosion by waves.

The eroding waves are the work of storms. In the two thousand years since Caesar first saw England—a mere blink in geological time—the English coastline in some places has moved 2 miles (3 km) inland.

In other parts of the world, fishing villages that prospered in colonial times now find themselves landlocked. That could be the effect of silt brought down by a nearby river. But other mechanisms can bring about the same result.

A prevailing wind that strikes a coastline at an angle starts and maintains a current along the shore. Such a current may carry sand away from a crumbling headland. A sand spit starts. It will grow as the conveyor delivers more material day after day. Sandy Hook, at the southern entrance to New York is a good example of such a spit. That particular spit is not likely to grow until it closes off New York from the sea. At its tip tidal currents remove just about as much material as the along-shore current delivers.

But in other places a bay may become totally landlocked by such a spit. Or barrier islands may form by a similar process. Miami Beach and Galveston stand on such islands. Or look at the string of barrier islands, barely separated from each other, in the Cape Hatteras area.

But the wind's action in changing the map is totally insignificant compared with its role in creating the climate. Much more than half the land surface of the world gets more heat during one year from the sun than it radiates back to space. Without winds that area would get hotter year after year.

Most of the remaining land areas—including more than half of the United States—operate on an annual energy deficit. These areas would get colder year by year and soon be buried under sheets of ice like the interior of Antarctica.

Without winds to distribute heat surplus to deficit areas, only two narrow belts—one in the northern, one in the southern hemisphere, where energy income just balances outgo—would have temperatures suitable for plants and animals.

Worse. Without winds, rain and snow would fall only where there was water to create local clouds. Most of the land where the temperatures were tolerable would be deserts.

As it is, the wind makes temperatures over most of the land tolerable for at least some plants and animals, if only for a short season. Ocean currents help. Example: The Gulf Stream and its offspring, the Atlantic Drift, raise temperatures in the British Isles and moderate the climate of the Norwegian coast. These currents are caused by the wind. Steady easterly winds pile up water in the Gulf of Mexico. From there the warmed water runs downhill, urged on later by the prevailing westerly winds.

The winds also spread the moisture, most of which is evaporated over the oceans that cover seven tenths of the globe. The winds do that job of distribution so well that only a small percentage of the total land area gets less than 10 inches (25 cm) of rainfall a year, which classifies it as desert.

Moderate temperatures, moisture, and soil—some of that ground down or deposited by the wind—allow plants to grow on land. And all land animals, past and present, depend on plants for food. They either eat plants directly, as cows do, or eat plant-eaters, as an eagle does when he gets a rabbit.

Man uses both methods, having potatoes and salad with his grass-fed steak. And since the beginning of time man has used plants for other purposes: as raw material for shelters and fibers, oils and medicines, dyes and tanning agents.

And what has all that to do with the wind? A lot. In still air a seed would fall straight down and could only compete with its mother plant for light, moisture, and minerals. Few of the seedlings would win the fight. Forests and grasslands would never have spread. After floods, or fires caused by lightning, fertile lands would remain barren.

The wind is, without doubt, the greatest spreader of seeds. It may deflect a falling seed only a few inches or a few feet, just far enough to get it away from the mother plant. Or it may carry a dandelion seed equipped for hang-gliding a few city blocks, right into your front lawn. (There are of course other cunning mechanisms for spreading seeds. Castor beans are catapulted; sandspurs travel on Argyle socks. . . .)

But before there is a seed there must be pollination. The pollen must somehow reach the ovules.

Self-pollination—the transfer of pollen within the same flower, or from another flower of the same plant, is possible. But nature puts a premium on cross-pollination, fertilization by pollen from another plant. To that end she employs many different mechanisms.

In the date palm tree she separates the sexes. Some trees only produce pollen; other trees bear the fruit. Or she separates them within one flower in time. When the pollen is ready, the ovules aren't (in the daisy); or the other way round (in the horse chestnut).

In other plants nature has arranged for self-sterility. Fruit will not set unless pollinated by another plant. In other plants the taboo is not so strong. If the normal cross-pollination has not been achieved, the stamen curls as the flower fades and deposits its pollen in the right place.

When you hear about pollination, you probably think first of the honeybee and its relatives. But many other critters carry pollen from one plant to another: butterflies, hummingbirds, even bats and snails, and in a greenhouse a sable brush wielded by a human hand.

The most important pollinator is not vegetal, nor animal. It is the wind. All conifers (pines, firs, and such) count on the wind to do the job; so do oaks, alders, and birches. Also grasses—and their cultivated offspring the grains—sedges, and rushes. And ragweed and a lot of other plants, as hayfever sufferers sneezily know.

Pollen to be distributed by the wind is nonsticky, unlike the pollen that's supposed to stick to legs and rumps of bees. It is so fine as to be barely visible. But shake just one male pine cone at the right time and you loosen a cloud. You'll often see such pollen coating the still surface of a pond with a film of dust from shore to shore.

Many animals undoubtedly owe their distribution to the wind. Deer will move into an area recently reforested by that great seed carrier. Others, say insects and birds, may have been carried willy-nilly to regions new to their species. Even lizards and frogs have been seen "falling from the sky."

3

Wind and Man

This is a book about wind, not about climate. I don't have to write, and you don't have to read about the influence of climate on man.

That would get us into the thorny problem of national character and climate. Something already Hippocrates, two generations ahead of Aristotle, tried to tackle. Why are the Greeks different from the Barbarians? The question is still being debated. Can you explain the intellectual hustle of Europe and China by their wide annual swings in temperature, while in areas of more even temperatures few great inventions were made, few great books written?

Neither do we have to worry about another controversial question: Are the differences in human races caused by climatic differences?

I don't even have to write about the influence of *weather* on man. Don't you feel good on a sunny spring day? Blue under lowering skies?

But what about the wind?

Everybody knows the difference between the discomforts caused by wind-driven rain, snow, or sand and rain and snow falling straight down, sand lying still.

Everybody also knows that a breeze, even a light breeze, makes a hot day more bearable. That's why indoors you turn on a fan. It doesn't cool the air, but it cools your skin by increasing its rate of evaporation.

At the other end of the temperature scale, a cold wind blows right through your clothes, removes the body-warmed air between your skin and clothes, and the air trapped in the clothes themselves.

When that happens, your body has to heat more air. If it can't do so at the same rate as heat is lost, you feel cool, cold, or bitterly cold. You can protect your body with layers of warm clothes and an outer cover of windproof material. But if your ears and cheeks are unprotected, the skin there can't keep up with the heat loss. You'll get frostbite.

A thermometer hasn't got that problem. It indicates the same temperature regardless of wind velocity. To warn people of the danger of frostbite on exposed skin, the weather people use a wind-chill table. From that table you'll learn, for example, that the above-freezing temperature of 35° F with a wind of 10 miles per hour will turn your ears white and numb as quickly as still air at 21° F. With a 20-mile wind the effect on your exposed ears is the same as that of still air at 12° F.

(In metric units: Air of +2° C with a wind of 15 kilometers per hour will cause frostbite as quickly as still air at −5° C. With a 30-kilometer wind the effect on bare skin is the same as that of still air at −11° C.)

The wind has more subtle influences on man. More subtle and less understood than the freezing of your cheeks. It influences people's moods and actions.

A classic example: The sirocco, a warm southern wind in the Mediterranean unsettles and irritates almost everybody, some people more than others. If you pick your day to kill your wife, or a neighbor in piddling argument, your lawyer in some town on the Adriatic may get you off by "pleading the sirocco."

Winds have played fate in the lives of many people; not just unusual winds such as hurricanes and tornadoes. And not just the lives of seamen and shipowners. Think of the thousands of American farmers whose very soil took to the air in the 1930s.

Sometimes the winds have decided the history of whole nations.

We know the vast influence of Greek philosophy and knowledge on all Western thought. Much of that inheritance reached us through complicated lines: Egypt, Rome, Arabs in Spain, and scribes copying manuscripts in medieval monasteries.

What if the Persians had won the struggle that pitted mono-lithic imperialism against Greek city-state liberty on and off for one hundred years?

Many historians consider the sea battle off Salamis the turning point of that long war. The disastrous battle of Marathon, ten years earlier, had convinced the Persian high command that only a full-scale amphibious operation could subdue Greece. Xerxes' fleet was finally ready in 480 B.C. His ships far outnumbered and outweighed the Greek fleet. In open waters the Greek navy didn't have a chance.

The Greek Congress, a federation of thirty Greek states united for the purpose of defeating the Persians, decided to keep the fleet at Salamis, near Athens.

When Themistocles, the commander-in-chief of the allied naval forces, informed the captains of that decision, most of them were unhappy. They wanted to retreat to the Argolic Gulf.

Themistocles saw to it that Xerxes heard about their desire. A perfectly logical desire in the face of a superior enemy. During the night Xerxes detached 200 of his ships to cut that line of retreat. He stationed his remaining 1,200 ships off the Straits of Salamis.

Sure enough, in the morning Xerxes saw some Greek ships seemingly trying to escape. It was already September, the end of the good weather season. A decisive battle was needed and needed soon. So he ordered his main fleet into the strait. Right into the trap Themistocles had set.

Themistocles, who had detached a small force to deal with the 200 Persian vessels, kept his remaining 310 ships out of sight. These ships, most of them supplied by Athens, propelled by three banks of oars, were built for ramming. Their keels projected under the bows and ended in a sharp point designed to hole an enemy ship below the waterline.

In the straits the Persian ships lacked maneuvering room. Oars-men on one vessel locked oars with its neighbor. Before the mess was sorted out a third ship piled into the tangle. Then another. The confusion among the Persian ships reached a climax when the morning sea breeze sprang up, making the narrow strait choppy. Just as Themistocles had expected. That's when he or-dered the attack.

The Persian ships that could extricate themselves turned and set sail for Asia.

Had the Persian fleet prevailed, would there have been a Plato, an Aristotle, a Euclid? Who can tell?

In 1259 or 1260 Kublai Khan, a grandson of Genghis Khan, became the head of the Mongol empire. Before long that empire was to stretch from Poland and Arabia to the Pacific, and Kublai Khan would be emperor of all China.

Like all conquerors—from Alexander, through Napoleon, to Hitler—Kublai Khan, a master of psychological warfare, frightened unconquered regions into subservience. Korea had been an early victim of that tactic. Japan, a mere one hundred nautical miles across the strait from Pusan, was next on the list.

A half-dozen missions sent to Japan achieved nothing. Something had to be done. The Mongols were horse people, unskilled in shipbuilding and seafaring. So the king of Korea was ordered to build a fleet of warships and man them. In 1274 the invasion force set sail. Quite a force: some forty thousand men (eight times the number of William the Conqueror's contingent) in three hundred large ships supported by at least three hundred smaller vessels.

They had no trouble overwhelming the Japanese garrisons on the off-lying islands. Then on November 17 they began to land on Kyushu, the southernmost of the main islands that make up Japan. Their crossbows greatly outranged the samurai's weapons. Some historians believe the invaders also used rockets.

Two days after the first landing it looked as if the entire Japanese force on Kyushu would be wiped out before reinforcements from Honshu, the main island, could be brought in.

That night the weather-wise Korean sea captains saw the signs of a storm in the sky. Their advice to the generals: "Re-embark the troops immediately. The ships will drag ashore when the storm hits."

By the first light of dawn the Japanese saw the last of the enemy ships standing out of Hakata Bay. One vessel ran aground before getting to sea; many more sank in the strait. Korean records tell of thirteen thousand men and two hundred vessels lost.

The Khan convinced himself that it had been the storm that had caused the failure of the invasion. You can't see his generals arguing him out of that. So next year he sent another delegation to Japan asking for submission. The Japanese commander had the emissaries executed.

Even the psychological effect of the submission of southern China, and its increase in ships and fighting men failed to budge the Japanese. In 1281 a force larger than the first was raised in Korea; another invasion force from China, said to have numbered a hundred thousand men, was to rendezvous at sea with the northern invasion fleet. The operation was undoubtedly timed to be completed before the typhoon season that begins in late summer and reaches its peak in the early fall. But the southern fleet was not ready until late June.

The Korean fleet again entered Hakata Bay; the Chinese contingent established a beachhead in a bay farther south on the same coast, just north of Nagasaki.

The northern army ran into fortifications built since the last invasion attempt. The heart of the Chinese soldiers may not have been in fighting for their new Mongol overlords. Anyway, the Japanese forces managed to contain both beachheads for six weeks.

Then on August 15 and 16 a typhoon—a Pacific hurricane—struck Kyushu. Some ships sailed without loading troops. Others made it out of the bay only to be smashed against the shore of an island no more than four miles away. Most of the ships that escaped were overwhelmed by wind and waves in the strait.

Marco Polo, who was counselor to Kublai Khan at that time, writes that only thirty thousand—less than one third of the original force—survived.

In Japanese history this storm became known as *Kamikaze* (divine wind). But for that wind, Japan might have been a Chinese province for the last seven hundred years.

The year is 1588. The invincible Armada sets sail from Lisbon for England.

The execution of Mary Queen of Scots the year before has dashed the hope of Philip II of Spain for a Catholic successor to the throne of Elizabeth I. Drake's raids—on the Spanish colonies in America and just last year on Cadiz in Spain itself—and Elizabeth's help to the rebellious Netherlands have been too much. Philip sees but one solution: invasion of England.

His conquest of Portugal a few years earlier has given him many additional ships and skilled mariners. But still not enough for an invasion directly from Spain. (His chiefs of staff had estimated that that would take six hundred ships and a hundred thousand men.)

The new plan sounds simple. Have the Armada destroy the English fleet. Then have the troops under the Duke of Parma invade across the channel using the ships as transports from Dunkerque.

Philip's admirals have seen Drake in action. Against his fast-sailing, quick-turning ships, oar power, on which most of the Spanish warships still depend, would be useless. So the Armada is made up of ships that can fight under sail: 24 men-of-war and the best merchant vessels of Spain and Portugal converted for fighting; 130 ships in all.

The Spanish commanders propose to use the time-tested strategy of boarding. Proof: Soldiers in their ships outnumber sailors by more than two to one. To destroy the English fleet they rely mainly on cannons that can hurl a round of shot weighing up to 50 pounds (23 kg).

On July 29 the Armada makes its landfall at the Lizard, at the western entrance to the English Channel. The English fleet is at Plymouth, fifty nautical miles to the east. It cannot sail. The wind is in the wrong quarter. But sailors at the oars of longboats tow some of the sitting ducks out of the harbor. Other ships have their longboats carry out an anchor and drop it. Then the crew winches the ship toward the anchor. When the anchor breaks out, it is carried out again and the winching starts all over.

When all the ships are clear of the harbor and to windward of the enemy, the English attack. Their culverines fire light shot— average weight 7 pounds (3 kg)—that far outranges the heavy Spanish missiles. So the English ships simply stay out of range of the Spanish cannon. They do that so well that there is no damage to any of their ships. But neither does the light English shot penetrate the Spanish hulls.

As the Spanish fleet lumbers upchannel, the English vessels follow, staying upwind. Off Portland Bill the English attack again: few losses, little damage to the enemy. The same result during the engagements of the next two days off the Isle of Wight.

In all these engagements the Spanish cannot turn and sail into the wind to close the gap and bring their heavier guns to bear. So in defensive formation they keep bumbling upchannel to make contact with Parma.

On the eve of August 7 the Spanish fleet anchors off Calais, on the French side of the Channel. At midnight the English, still upwind, launch six burning ships to drift toward the Armada. None starts a fire. But the Spanish captains panic. "Cut the anchor cables." Their ships drift eastward without any semblance of formation. The English follow, intensify their harassing fire. The Spanish ships keep firing their cannon to keep the enemy from closing range.

Then one by one the Spanish guns fall silent. Out of round shot. The English ships close in. Now their light guns take their toll. They batter the flagship, sink at least three men-of-war, dismast some vessels, open leaks in many more.

Then they too run out of shot. But the Armada looks finished anyway. The northwest wind pushes it ever closer to the lee shore and certain shipwreck.

Now the wind backs suddenly into the southwest.

Although the invasion plan is ruined—the fleet is well past the region controlled by the Duke of Parma—the fleet can still save itself. The plan: Sail home through the North Sea and around Scotland.

But the wind, which by its sudden shift has saved the Armada from shipwreck, is only playing cat-and-mouse. Many ships lacking masts, sails, food, water, even anchors and cables, never make it to Scotland. Others are wrecked by a storm off the Irish coast. More than fifty ships and nine thousand men never reach home.

A historian might comment that the engagements between the Spanish Armada and the English fleet were the first sea battles fought between ships entirely driven by wind after more than two thousand years of ships that relied in battle on oars.

Other historians date the expansion of British sea power from the victory over the then-dominant sea power, Spain.

In simpler terms: The wind that week could have shifted briefly to some easterly quadrant. That would have put the pursued Spanish fleet to windward. And you might now read this book in Spanish.

4

Measuring the Wind

You can describe the direction of a wind well enough for everyday conversation: up the valley, from the lake, right from the fertilizer plant. . . . In the same way you may describe its strength (or force, or speed): calm (that is, nonexistent), light, stiff, howling. . . .

But a weather forecast is not likely to read, "Tomorrow it's going to blow like stink, from Canada." Weathermen—and authors of books on wind—have to be more precise. So in this chapter I'll talk about measuring and expressing wind direction and speed. Direction first.

It was always easy to tell which way the wind blew. Before the introduction of the magnetic compass the problem was to *name* that direction. In ancient Athens you might have said, "It blows from the direction of the sun's shadow at noon." Clumsy. So you simply called the wind "Boreas."

As a public service, the city fathers of Athens had an eight-sided tower built, each side decorated with a picture and the name of one wind. A vane on top of that structure turned with the wind; when it blew from the north, it would indicate Boreas.

Eight winds are still enough for most purposes. We have made it easier for ourselves—and less poetic—by calling them simply by eight points of the compass. The four cardinal points, north, east, south, and west, and the four points in between. In naming these in-between points we always put north or south first: northeast, southeast, southwest, and northwest. The abbreviations are obvious: N, E, S, W and NE, SE, SW, NW.

For most purposes these eight directions are good enough, mainly because on most days and in most places the wind doesn't come steadily from one direction. You'll see the wind vane yaw, pointing now a little to one side, now to the other.

But you can refine the direction. You could call a wind between north and northeast a north-northeast (NNE) wind; one between east and northeast you could call an east-northeast (ENE) wind. That's the system the Weather Service uses in climatological summaries. Example: The prevailing wind direction at Key West in November is given as ENE. For reporting the wind and plotting daily weather maps, the Weather Service uses the nearest 10 degrees (counted from north, clockwise). ENE becomes 70°.

As in ancient Greece, we name the wind after the direction *from* which it blows. The (usually cold) north wind is supposed to come from the cold north; the (usually warm) south wind is thought to come from the warm south.

That seems entirely logical. But ocean currents are named the other way, after the direction *in* which they flow. Off Florida the Gulf Stream sets north. When a north wind blows over it—opposing the stream's direction—it creates minor hell for small craft, and craft not so small.

For many centuries wind vanes were mounted on church steeples and public buildings, and everybody knew their orientation. Your neighbor's weathercock probably sits above a base clearly marked N, E, S, and W. And most cities and towns in the United States and Canada are laid out so that streets or avenues follow these compass directions.

Away from home, if you use a compass, don't forget it indicates *magnetic* north, not true north. The north indicated by a magnetic compass in Maine is really NNW, in the state of Washington it's really NNE. If the difference between magnetic and true north—called *variation* by sailors, *declination* by landsmen—is only a few degrees, it's not worth bothering about for telling wind direction.

My usual weather vane is the flag that flies over a military cemetery across the street. On very windy days, when to save wear the flag is not raised, I look at the palm trees.

Smoke is a good wind indicator. But some stacks are now so tall

—to better spread the pollution—that they indicate the wind at high level, where its direction is usually different from the wind near the ground.

Out of doors, when the wind is so gentle that it's hard to tell where it comes from, people wet one finger and hold it up. Where it feels coolest, that's where the wind comes from. (Turning your head until you feel the wind on the back of *both* ears works for shorthairs.)

I once sailed with a first mate who before entering the wind direction in the log wet and held up one finger *inside* the chartroom. Visitors were supposed to object. But he had been on duty for four hours. Even if he had never stepped onto the open part of the bridge, he knew exactly which way the wind blew. How? By observing the wavelets created by the local wind. (Not the big waves or swells caused by distant winds.)

That's the proper way to check the wind direction on a moving vessel. The ribbons and miniature wind socks you see on sailboats, and my large ears, respond to the *apparent* wind, a combination of the true wind and the headwind created by the motion of your vessel. (On the boat deck of the *Queen Elizabeth 2* you'd feel a moderate gale from dead ahead on a totally windless day.)

In a sailboat one way to get the true wind direction is to look at the compass when she is "going through the wind" when you are tacking. When the sails go limp, just before the boom swings over, her true heading is the wind direction. To get the true heading from the compass, you have to apply, of course, the variation and any deviation (compass error on that heading on *your* vessel).

Thomas Jefferson, who kept systematic weather records, didn't like to have to step outside. So he installed a weather vane with a long shaft that ran through the roof, through an upstairs room, and down to his study, where it indicated the wind direction. You can still see it in Monticello. Today every yacht club worth its martinis has a remote-reading wind indicator in which the creaky shaft has been replaced by an electric gadget.

At the weather office they have gone one step further. A wind vane—shaped like a miniature airplane and brought into the wind by its tail assembly—transmits an electrical signal into the office. There it works a pen under which a strip of paper, driven by a clock mechanism, slowly moves from one cylinder to another. Result: a permanent record of the ever-changing wind direction at that station.

Getting the direction of the wind and talking about it is really simple. But how about the strength of the wind?

Description soon runs into difficulty. Say you pick terms like breeze, gale, storm. . . . Not everyone will agree which is stronger, a gale or a storm. When you add qualifiers such as moderate, fresh, strong . . . where does one leave off and the next begin? Can you call any horribly strong wind a hurricane, or is that word to be reserved only for a certain type of storm? Now it's reserved. That's why you so often hear the apparently clumsy description "winds of hurricane force."

To get more specific, you could build a simple gadget: a hinged plate turned into the wind by you or, simpler, by a weather vane. The plate would lift according to the strength of the wind—much as laundry on the line droops in a calm and stands out at an angle when the wind blows. You could measure the angle of tilt in degrees. Or you could assign it numbers from 0 for calm to, say, 10 for the highest wind the gadget could stand. Anyone with the same apparatus would know just how strong the wind blew.

I had never thought of such a wind-measuring instrument when I had to show in a photograph for a magazine article just how strong the wind had been blowing.

It was a wind you won't encounter in many places. A whole gale or worse with a clear sky and a moderate sea. A photographer's delight. This wind, called a Tehuantepecer, hit our freighter—where else?—in the Gulf of Tehuantepec on the Pacific coast of Mexico. The sky was clear because this wind, unlike most, is not caused by some traveling weather disturbance. Instead it is the sudden flushing of air, dammed up by the Sierra Madre, through a low pass. We were too close to the coast for the wind to whip up the sea.

The mate, not one to coddle his crew, decided that was a good day to paint the top of the mast. I could not show the paint blowing off the paintbrush without climbing the mast, something I'm most reluctant to do at any time. Instead I showed the rope used to haul up paint standing out almost horizontally against a heavily filtered sky. The shot turned out beautifully and I was proud of my wind gauge. Postscript: The editor, to conserve space, cropped the picture closely, leaving two unexplained Irish pennants untidily running out of the picture.

Wind instruments based on the lifting power of the wind never became popular. Instead, in 1806, the world was given by Admiral Sir Francis Beaufort (the first syllable rhymes with blow) a table describing winds on a scale of 0 to 12. Originally this table was based on the sails a British frigate would carry with such a wind. It made sense for the navy. Every officer had at one time served in a frigate and knew what wind force would make the captain order to take a reef in a given sail, or take it in.

The Beaufort table has been revised in many ways. It was, for instance, adapted to the sails carried by a Thames barge. But now you don't always have a frigate or a Thames barge in sight. So now at sea you use the state of the sea itself for reference. Example: When whitecaps first appear, you'd log force 3; when white foam from breaking waves begins to be blown in streaks you'd log force 7.

"Force" really should be in quotation marks. The scale is not based on a force in the sense that that word is used in physics. Nor is force-4 wind twice—or four times—as strong as wind of force 2.

On a moving vessel wind speed measured by any instrument is again an apparent speed. It's again a combination of the true wind and the wind created by the progress of your craft. When you are steaming before the wind and at the same speed as the wind, you'll record no wind at all. The smoke will rise perfectly straight up. Moving into the wind at the same speed, your instruments would register twice the true wind speed. That's what makes the use of the state of the sea for measuring the wind the simplest method.

The Beaufort scale has also been adapted to use on land. Example: Leaves and twigs in constant motion translate into force 3; whole trees in motion indicate force 7.

Beaufort numbers now are of little interest. Wind strength is universally expressed as speed.

By international agreement weather services around the world use the knot as the basic unit of wind speed. The knot—one nautical mile per hour—is a truly international unit. Everybody uses the same hours, and the nautical mile is not based on either the English or the metric system. Instead it is equal to one minute of latitude, measured halfway between the equator and either pole. It's equivalent to about 6,076 feet or exactly 1,852 meters.

A nautical mile is about 15 per cent longer than the more familiar statute mile. That happens to deliver a fringe benefit. Over water, above the wave level, winds normally blow about 15 per cent faster than on land at the usual height of measurement. So a forecaster in a coastal area predicting 10- to 15-knot winds over water, can forecast 10- to 15-mile-per-hour winds over his land area.

A reader familiar with speeds in statute miles per hour from driving an automobile may want to add 15 per cent to convert knots to miles per hour. For low wind speeds that's hardly necessary. A 20-knot wind is a 23-mph wind. Without a measuring instrument you couldn't tell it from a 20-mph wind. On any wind gauge it would probably read 20 mph one minute, 23 the next. But at really high wind speeds the difference becomes appreciable. A 100-knot (115-mph) hurricane may take off with your roof that would have stayed in place in a 100-mph hurricane.

Readers used to kilometers per hour can convert knots to km/h by multiplying by 1.852. A quick way to do that is to double the speed in knots, then take off 10 per cent. Example: 20 knots becomes $40 - 4 = 36$ km/h. (Exact calculation would give 37 km /h.) For low speeds simply doubling the speed in knots is probably good enough. A 40-km/h (20-knot) wind feels no different than a 37-km/h wind. On an instrument it may register 40 km/h one minute, 37 the next.

There is another standard unit of wind speed, meters per second. You may encounter it in textbooks on meteorology. One m/sec equals 2 knots; one knot equals 0.5 m/sec. That's accurate to within about 3 per cent, probably more accurate than any wind gauge. And since wind speeds change all the time, absolute accuracy in conversion has little meaning anyway.

Beaufort numbers can be translated into wind speed. For example: Force 3, the sailor's gentle breeze, corresponds to 7–10 knots.

Force 7, the sailor's moderate gale, corresponds to winds of 28–33 knots.

In this book wind speeds will be given mainly in knots. If you prefer to think in other units, you won't be far off if you use the following conversion:

> 1 knot = 1 nautical mile per hour
> = very roughly 1 statute mile per hour (mph)
> = roughly 2 kilometers per hour (km/h)
> = about 0.5 meter per second (m/s)

If you insist on greater precision, here are the conversion figures:

INTERNATIONAL UNITS	ENGLISH UNITS	METRIC UNITS
1 knot (nautical mile per hour, kn)	1.15 statute miles per hour (mph)	1.85 kilometers per hour (km/h)
1 meter per second (m/s)	1.94 knots (kn)	3.60 kilometers per hour (km/h)
	2.24 miles per hour (mph)	

The best-known instrument for measuring wind speed is the cup anemometer. Its three, four, or five cups—in the shape of cones or half-spheres—rotate in the horizontal plane. What makes them turn? The pressure of the wind is about three times greater on the open side than on the more streamlined side. The stronger the wind, the faster the cups whirl. You could attach a counter to the rotating shaft or a mechanical speedometer similar to the one in your automobile. Usually the cups drive a small electric generator that is connected to a meter in the weather bureau or the bar of the yacht club.

In another model a propeller on a device that looks like a toy airplane drives the generator. That's the same airplane that, turned into the wind by its tail, measures and transmits the direction of the wind.

You can let the output of the wind-speed generator work a pen over a clock-driven strip of paper. From that record you can read the average wind speed, and the speed (and exact time) of the highest gusts. That's the type of installation you'll find at a weather office.

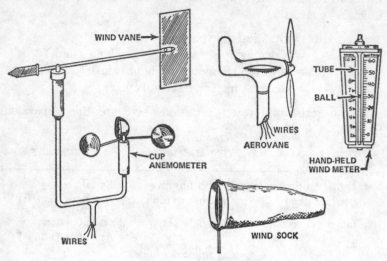

1. Measuring the wind

For your own use, if you don't mind stepping outside, there is a hand-held instrument in which a small turbine replaces the cups, and which shows wind speed on a dial in knots or miles per hour. You'll find it advertised in boating magazines.

In marine hardware stores you'll find the very simple Dwyer wind meter, which sells for a few dollars. In that instrument the wind lifts a little ball inside a six-inch long tube. The stronger the wind, the higher the ball rises. You read the wind speed from one of two scales. With the top of the tube open it reads up to 10 mph; with the tube covered with your finger, it reads up to 66 mph. (A test I performed with one of these meters by holding it above the windshield of an open car showed good agreement with the car's speedometer.)

You probably won't care to step outside when the wind exceeds that speed (57 knots). Even the Weather Service has trouble measuring high wind speeds. The highest winds in most hurri-

Do Not

TOUCH

Katie Collins

James A. Boyle, Sr.

e house

re

ean kitchen floor."

10 Quotes -
things significant
to Pip's death -
who said them - pg.
what signif.

Mr. Bright
for this
Webster

Magwitch

Wemmick

Cover tag?

canes are never recorded. Instead we find the notation "Instrument failed." Sometimes, to relieve the monotony of instrument failures, the entry reads, "Mast blown away." And in one report I read a brief "Station blown away."

5

More Measuring:

Temperature and

Atmospheric Pressure

Even without instruments you can, as we have seen, describe the direction and speed of a wind. But describing the warmth or coldness of a wind—including a zero-speed wind, calm air—isn't easy.

Our skin is very sensitive to temperature. But people's sense of hot, comfortable, and cold differ widely. What seems warm to one person is chilly to another. That's the cause of much fiddling with thermostats, and the reason for dual controls on electric blankets. People who come to southern Florida in winter find the ocean delightful for swimming; the skin of Floridians, remembering the ocean in summer, goes into shock even in a heated pool.

When you step from your air-conditioned house onto the veranda, it seems hot; coming in from the sun, you feel cool on the same veranda. The lecturer, "warming to his subject," and perhaps pacing and waving his arms, takes off his coat; the students sitting still, and bored, shiver. You were chilly before dinner; now at the same thermostat setting you feel toasty. While you wait in the wind for your bus, you hear your teeth chatter; in the telephone booth—where the temperature can't be very different—you feel passably comfortable.

Conceivably weathermen could be found whose heat-cold sensations would match those of the majority of people. At just the right state of digestion, and without warming to the subject, they could report air temperature from a telephone booth. They could use a code of nine universally agreed terms to describe temperature, ranging perhaps from extremely bloody cold to incredibly stinking hot.

That might do for reporting. But for *explaining* the winds, and perhaps forecasting them, they'll need more accurate information. To put it differently: Before meteorology could become a science, it was necessary to *measure* temperatures, not just speculate that the sun's fast and near motion caused wind as Aristotle had done.

Galileo Galilei (1564–1642) would have been one of the first to agree with that statement. I don't mean only that he would have been most eager to endorse that thought. He also was one of the earliest of Western minds to feel the necessity for numbers rather than logical principles.

He was the man who, according to legend, dropped a cannon ball and a wooden ball of the same size to time their fall. Every scientist *knew* the heavier ball would fall faster. Aristotle had said so. But when Galileo dropped both balls at the same moment, he saw them land at the same instant.

I don't know how he proposed to time the falling balls. Perhaps by counting. Perhaps with a pendulum. For it was also he who had observed that a weight on a string always takes the same time to complete one swing. When you first start a pendulum swinging, it moves rapidly through a large arc; when it's about to die, it moves slowly in a small arc. The time of each swing is the same. It depends only on the length of the string and not the attached weight, nor the angle of swing. (He even suggested that principle for the regulation of a mechanical clock. But it was fifty years before someone built the first one.)

It is probably not true that he dropped the balls off the leaning tower in Pisa, but it makes a good story and reminds you where he lived. He may not have gotten the pendulum idea by watching the chandelier in church. Did he invent the thermometer, as you may have learned in school?

Well, not exactly. The apparatus he designed has been called a thermoscope, literally something that lets you see heat. Is that a quibble? Let's see.

His device was simple: a glass tube, open at both ends, sealed into a container partly filled with a liquid (colored to make it easier to see). When you had blown more air into the container through the free end of the tube, the colored liquid rose part way up the tube.

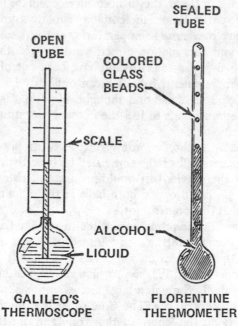

2. Measuring temperature. Left: Galileo's thermoscope; right: Florentine thermometer

When you warmed the apparatus, say by putting your hand on the container, the liquid in the tube rose. When you withdrew your hand and the container had cooled to room temperature, the colored liquid returned to its former level.

You can readily see what happened. The air in the container expanded when your hand heated it and contracted to its former volume after you took your hand away. An attached scale made it all look very scientific.

There was one hitch. On the next day the liquid stood at a different level in the tube. Explanation: The air pressure in Pisa had changed; the pressure in the container had not. Galileo had also built a barometer.

Not long after Galileo's death, glass blowers in Florence made, as far as we know, the first thermometers that worked. As in modern thermometers, the bulb contained no air and the top of the tube was closed. The liquid itself, expanding and contracting, indicated the temperature. Interestingly, the liquid was alcohol, still used in thermometers for its low freezing point. The scale, in the form of colored glass beads, was fused directly to the tube.

The original scale was arbitrary. Some standard scale was needed. The one English-speaking people know best is that of Gabriel Daniel Fahrenheit, an instrument maker born in Danzig, who lived most of his life in Holland. On his scale 0° is 32 degrees below the freezing (or melting) point of water. Why? You may have heard that zero degrees was the coldest it ever got where he lived. Nonsense. A thermometer maker needs a temperature he can reproduce at any time. Fahrenheit mixed coarse salt and crushed ice—as in a home ice-cream maker—and that was his zero point.

Somewhat earlier Isaac Newton had proposed a scale on which the freezing point of water was taken as 0°, the temperature of a healthy person as 12°. Twelve sounded like such a nice English unit, as in twelve inches to the foot. Perhaps Fahrenheit saved us from having to tell the doctor that baby's temperature was 12⅝°. To get away from such fractions, he is said to have chosen eight times twelve, 96°, as normal body temperature, about 3 degrees below the true value. By the way, he was aware of the boiling point of water at sea level at 212° F.

In practical use in most of the world, and by scientists everywhere, is another scale. Its 0 is the temperature of melting ice; the interval to the boiling point of water is divided into 100 degrees—not 180 as on the Fahrenheit scale. That's why it was often called the centigrade ("hundred degree") scale. The official name now is the Celsius scale and the degrees are called degrees Celsius (°C) after Anders Celsius, the Swedish astronomer who proposed the scale.

(To confuse everybody, a Frenchman, R. A. F. de Réaumur, proposed a scale where the same interval was divided into 80 de-

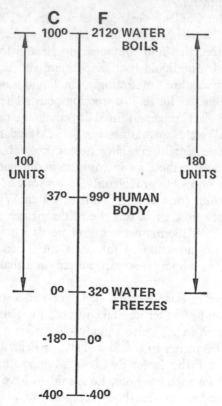

3. Thermometer scales, Celsius and Fahrenheit

grees. That system, which has nothing whatever to recommend it, is now obsolete.)

It's only a matter of time before the United States will officially use Celsius degrees. Canada does already. In this book I'll give temperatures on both scales to save you the trouble of converting.

Most thermometers are filled with mercury, which metal stays liquid at temperatures that concern most people. To measure air temperatures a thermometer must be shaded from the sun, as in the familiar louvered instrument shelter. To get the highest and lowest reading for a period, say one day, we use two thermometers, one indicating the minimum, the other the maximum temperature. (A fever thermometer is also a maximum thermometer; a narrowing in the tube lets the mercury rise but prevents its running back to the bulb.)

One can also read the highest and lowest temperature from the chart of a thermograph, an instrument that continuously records the air temperature.

In one model a strip of metal changes shape with changing temperature. That moves a pen up or down on a clock-driven roll of paper.

For remote reading or recording, electricity is used. The sensor may be an electric wire that changes resistance with temperature. You can send a similar sensor aloft in a balloon and have it radio the temperature at any height back to earth.

Before meteorology could become a science able to explain and perhaps forecast winds, at least one more tool had to be invented: the barometer.

We live at the bottom of an ocean of air. But we are totally unaware of the pressure that bears down on us. Why? Because the same pressure also pushes upward (and in all other directions), just as a fish in the ocean doesn't get pushed down—or in any other direction—by the water above it.

We are unaware of the pressure and seem to lack a sense for detecting its changes. Some people say they can feel when the "glass is low." Their joints ache, or their sinuses act up, or they get depressed. Perhaps the air pressure in their joints and head hasn't had a chance to equalize with the outer pressure and causes pain. Perhaps other phenomena that go with low and high barometer readings trigger the symptoms. With a high barometer we are likely to have pleasant, dry weather; with a low barometer low clouds and rain. That alone could somehow be responsible for a flare-up of arthritic pain, sinus trouble, and recurrence of depression.

In 1642 Galileo, seventy-eight years old, under house arrest for the preceding eight years, totally blind, and knowing his time was running out, found a younger man to whom to dictate his notes: Evangelista Torricelli. Torricelli, then thirty-nine, a mathematician and scientist, was of course familiar with Galileo's earlier work. In the three months remaining to Galileo did he discuss with Torricelli the failure of the thermoscope to reproduce temperature readings on successive days? Was that what set Torricelli off to investigate air pressure, sparked his invention of the barometer?

The apparatus was simple. You filled a glass tube, about a yard (meter) long and closed at one end, with mercury. Then you held your finger over the open end, turned the tube so the open end was down, and immersed the end in a tank also filled with mercury. When you withdrew your finger, the column of mercury dropped a little but always came to rest about 30 inches (76 cm) above the level of mercury in the tank.

It didn't matter whether the tube was held straight or slanted, it was the same height above the tank. You could also use a tube in the shape of a letter U or J. As long as one end of the tube was closed when full of mercury and the other open, the column dropped to the same level as in Torricelli's original design.

Torricelli gave the right explanation: The dropping mercury column created a vacuum in the closed tube. The pressure of air on the open surface—the tank or the open leg of the bent tube—balanced the weight of the column of mercury that had no air weighing down on it.

That ran against all established teaching. Ever since Aristotle, every scientist knew that water followed the piston in a pump because "nature abhors a vacuum."

Torricelli noted the change in level of the mercury column with changing weather. About an inch (a few centimeters) up or down. And he predicted that at higher elevations the level of mercury would be lower than in Florence, since less air would press down on the open surface.

Blaise Pascal, in France, soon proved that right. He made two

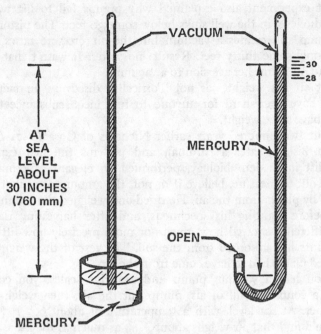

4. Measuring atmospheric pressure, mercury barometers

identical barometers and observed the level in one, while his brother-in-law carried the other one to the peak of Puy de Dôme, 4,806 feet (1,465 m) high. The moving barometer dropped steadily on the way up—several inches in all—rose steadily on the way down. The stationary barometer showed virtually no movement all that day.

Pascal performed another experiment that proved Torricelli's explanation right. He got a glass tube 40 feet (14 m) long, and—being a Frenchman—filled it with wine. The wine in the tube leveled out some thirty feet above the wine in the tank. If you filled such a tube with water when a mercury barometer reads 30 inches (760 mm), you would measure a height of about 34 feet (10.3 m). The column of water is 13.6 times longer than the column of mercury. And 13.6 is exactly the ratio of the weight of one quart (or liter) of mercury to the weight of one quart (or liter) of water.

That experiment also explained why pumps fail to lift water when the level in the well sinks below some 30 feet. The piston in the pump still creates a vacuum but the air pressure raises the water only some thirty feet. Result: no water. It wasn't that nature had overcome her aversion to a vacuum.

That air has weight was not Torricelli's discovery. In fact, it would have been hard for anyone to imagine a substance that didn't have some weight.

About two hundred years earlier Nicholas of Cusa (1401–64), then a bishop, later a cardinal, and perhaps the first experimentalist in modern biology, performed an elegant experiment. He set out to measure, believe it or not, the amount of weight absorbed by plants from the air. He dried and weighed the soil in his pots before planting his specimens, and after harvesting them. The difference showed how much—or more precisely how little— the plants had absorbed from the soil. The rest of the weight of his dried plants had to have come from the air.

If you had a vacuum pump and sensitive scales, you could weigh a container full of air, pump out the air, then weigh the container. At sea level, with a temperature of about 60° F (15° C) you'd find that air weighs about $\frac{1}{800}$ as much as the same volume of water.

That seems very light, but don't be misled. I just calculated the weight of such air in the room where I type this. The room is 13 by 20 feet, with an 8-foot ceiling. The air in the room weighs 159 pounds, a little more than I do. (For readers who think metric: The air in a similar room, 4 by 6 m, 2.5 m high, weighs about 73.5 kg, somewhat more than your author.)

The barometer does not measure what I have just calculated, the weight of air in a given volume. Instead it indicates the pressure exerted by a column of air reaching from the barometer to the top of the atmosphere. Of course there is no "top"; the air just gets thinner and thinner. At 100,000 feet (less than 20 miles or about 30 km) 99 per cent of all air molecules are already below you, only 1 per cent between you and the top.

Engineers refer to normal sea-level air pressure as one atmosphere. Since the pressure changes with altitude, temperature, and weather, in their calculations they use a standard atmosphere equal to a pressure of 14.7 pounds per square inch (1,033 kg per m²).

In meteorology an obvious choice was the length of a column of mercury that just balanced an air column of the same cross section. At sea level the annual temperature averages out to about 59° F (15° C), and at that temperature the air pressure at sea level is assumed to be normal at 29.92 inches (760 mm) of mercury.

Nobody seriously proposed to use some thirty feet of water, or wine. But water with color added was used in a standard household article of colonial times, the weather glass. The colored water rose and fell most interestingly in the short tube. Unfortunately it did so not only under the influence of lower and higher atmospheric pressure, but mainly according to the temperature. Someone had sold everybody a different version of Galileo's thermoscope. This one, supposed to show atmospheric pressure, showed temperature, while Galileo had had the opposite problem. Descendants of the original salesmen are still around. They now sell colonial weather glasses at outrageous prices as antiques.

Pressure is still expressed in inches (or millimeters) of mercury

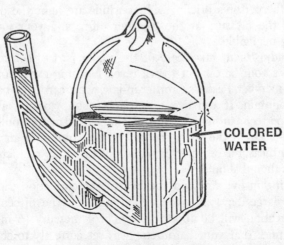

COLORED
WATER

5. Colonial weather glass

by people too young to have seen a mercury barometer. (The Weather Service still uses mercury barometers for calibration and checking of other instruments.) But for some years we were supposed to use another unit: millibars (mb). Standard pressure corresponding to 29.92 inches (760 mm) of mercury is 1,013.25 mb.

Even that unit, to which many of us haven't got used yet, is already obsolete for scientific use, but is still used by weather services. The basic unit to tie in with the *Système International* (SI) units, is the pascal. Before long, barometric pressure will be expressed as some multiple of that unit, as it is already in Canada. But cheer up. It will differ from the millibar only in name and placement of the decimal point. The standard pressure of 1,013.25 millibars may become 101.325 kilopascals (kPa). Perhaps for simplicity everybody will agree to use hectopascals (hPa). Then all that'll change will be the name; 1,013 mb will be called 1,013 hPa.

In whatever unit, the figure indicated by your barometer may be all wrong. On most dial barometers you can fix that. In the back you'll find a small screw. Turn it gently one way or the other and you'll see the needle move up or down. Adjust your barometer to agree with the reading given by a local radio or television station. Do that on a day of settled weather and low wind speed. (In settled weather the air pressure is not likely to have changed since the weatherperson's briefing; when winds are light the difference between the pressure at the weather office and your location is probably negligible.)

That adjustment takes care of the major part of correcting the reading of your barometer to sea level. Nothing mysterious about that. Remember Pascal's brother-in-law, who carried a barometer up a mountain. If you live 1,000 feet (about 300 m) above sea level, a perfect barometer without that adjustment would fail to take into account the last 1,000 feet of the column of air it is supposed to measure. It would show about one inch of mercury (34 mb) less than it should.

Even if you live right on the beach, the correction can be surprisingly large. Say you live in a highrise on the fifteenth floor. The correction will be about 0.17 inch of mercury (6 mb). And that assumes that your barometer was set correctly to start with.

The barometer in common use now is the *aneroid*, in which a flexible metal capsule (or bellows) drives the needle. The capsule expands when the atmospheric pressure drops, contracts when the pressure rises. That movement is very small and has to be mechanically magnified to drive the pointer over a large arc of the dial.

By itself the reading of a barometer, however accurate, is not of much use in forecasting the weather. Often it is more important to know whether the glass is rising or falling. The aneroid barometer makes that easy. Many such barometers have an extra hand you can set yourself. Set it to the present reading. When you look a few hours later, you'll notice whether the pressure has risen or fallen. The linkage between the pressure-sensitive capsule and the needle makes the pointer lag behind the change since the last reading. Tap the barometer and you'll see the needle rise or fall a little. That too is an indication of the pressure *tendency*. If you tap the barometer every time you read it, as you should, you'll soon be able to tell whether it's rising or falling, slowly or rapidly.

You can read that even better on a barograph, a recording barometer, in which a pressure-sensitive cell works a pen that traces the changing atmospheric pressure for a whole week on a ruled chart.

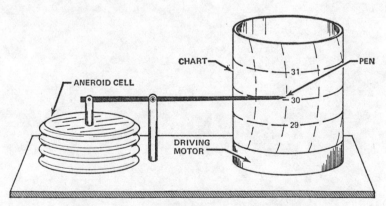

6. Recording barometer, barograph (simplified)

In the temperate zones such a barograph trace will show swings of about one inch of mercury (30 mb). In the tropics it will usually show a flat line with twice-daily tides. The pressure will be high around 10 A.M. and 10 P.M., low around 4 A.M. and 4 P.M. local time. These tides are of the order of 0.04 inch of mercury (1.5 mb).

There are several theories that explain these atmospheric tides. At present you wouldn't be far wrong in saying, "Their cause is a mystery."

6

And More Measuring:
Humidity, Etc.

Wind is air in motion. So you may expect me to give you some information about the composition of air. Compared to the label on a can of dog food, or a box of breakfast cereal, it is childishly simple. I'll make it even easier. I'll leave out, for the moment, the water contained in the atmosphere, and talk only about dry air.

Dry air, up to the level that interests you and me—say 50–60 miles (80–100 km) above sea level—shows the same composition everywhere in the world. That's how thoroughly the winds mix it. More than 99.96 per cent of dry air is made up of just three elements. In round figures:

Nitrogen	78%
Oxygen	21%
Argon	1%

You'll probably be surprised to find argon on the list, an element that wasn't discovered until 1894. And you may think I forgot carbon dioxide. I won't weasel out of that by saying it's not an element but a compound of carbon and oxygen. I don't have to. It only makes up about 0.03 per cent of the volume of dry air. So there you have it. The three common elements and carbon dioxide make up 99.99 per cent of the dry atmosphere.

You could look at it this way: Take a sample of air anywhere, dry it, and count the first 10,000 molecules. On the average you'd find 7,808 molecules of nitrogen, 2,095 of oxygen, 93 of argon, and only 3 of carbon dioxide. You'll have one molecule of some other gas left over. Most often that will be neon or helium.

If the air is the same up to great heights, why do pilots and mountaineers need bottled oxygen? The air gets thinner as you go up. Each breath contains fewer oxygen molecules than we are used to near the bottom of the atmosphere. We can't take much larger breaths or breathe much more often. So we give these people additional oxygen, or pressurize the cabin of an airplane, to restore the oxygen molecule count per breath to more normal levels.

How much air is there surrounding our planet?

Let's avoid the difficulty of having to visualize the air getting thinner and thinner as you go up. (At the top of Mount Everest—29,028 feet or 8,848 m—the pressure is down to about one third of sea-level pressure. About two thirds of the atmosphere is already below you; only one third is between you and space.)

Let's instead imagine the entire atmosphere uniformly pressurized and heated, to standard sea-level conditions. Such an imaginary atmosphere would reach to a height of only about 27,500 feet (8,400 m). Not even the height of Everest.

You can check that my calculation is about right. The water in Pascal's barometer, balanced by the entire column of air down to sea level rises to about 34 feet (10.4 m). We have seen that air at sea level is about 1/800 the weight of water. So the balancing uniform air column must be about eight hundred times as high as the column of water. With these rough figures you get 27,200 feet and 8,320 m.

While we are making such a mental experiment, we could also imagine that the various components of the air were miraculously separated into layers, like different liqueurs in a fancy drink.

The layer of nitrogen would be by far the thickest. More than 21,000 feet (6,500 m) high. That's about the height of Mount McKinley, the highest mountain in North America.

The oxygen layer would be not quite 6,000 feet (1,750 m) high. About the height of the highest peaks in the eastern United States.

The argon layer would be about 250 feet (75 m), about the height of a building of some twenty stories.

The carbon dioxide layer, about 8 feet (2.5 m) high, would just reach from your floor to the ceiling.

Toward the end of this book you'll read about some other gases in the atmosphere, and about solid particles suspended in the air. But now I'll talk about a most important part of the atmosphere: water.

You know, as Aristotle already knew, that water in the atmosphere comes in many forms. As a gas (invisible water vapor), as a liquid (the droplets in fog and low clouds), and as a solid (in ice crystals in high clouds, and in hailstones and snowflakes).

I have discussed dry air separately from water in the air for three reasons.

ONE: Unlike the gases that make up dry air and reach uniformly to great heights, water in all its forms, is virtually confined to the bottom of the atmosphere. In mid latitudes almost all of the water in the atmosphere is found below 36,000 feet (11 km). In the tropics it reaches higher, to about 49,000 feet (15 km); in the polar regions not quite so high, to about 30,000 feet (9 km).

TWO: In this wet zone the vertical distribution is very uneven. Near the ground you may have so much moisture in the air that it becomes visible as fog; above that is dry, cloudless sky.

THREE: The horizontal distribution of moisture also varies widely. Over a warm ocean or a tropical jungle water vapor may make up 3 per cent of the total volume of air; over arctic ice or a desert you'd measure a small fraction of 1 per cent.

We are vaguely aware of these differences. And you may notice that your toothbrush dries between brushings in Tucson, but doesn't in Seattle.

But we need better instruments than a toothbrush to measure the humidity in the air. The first such device was invented, around the year 1500, by Leonardo da Vinci. He took a ball of wool and weighed it on a jeweler's scale. On damp days it weighed more than on dry days.

Have you ever planned a camping trip in a national forest and been turned back by a ranger? How does the Forest Service decide when to close the woods? Mainly with a gadget made of a few sticks of wood. When the weight of the sticks drops below a cer-

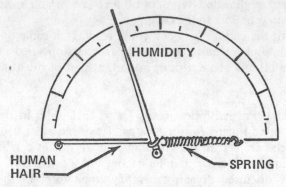

7. Measuring humidity, hygrometer (simplified)

tain level, the rangers know the hazard for forest fires to be critical.

In 1783 another instrument to measure the moisture in the air was invented. This *hygrometer* uses a human hair, washed in alcohol to remove its oil, and a spring to hold it taut. Between bone-dry air and maximum humidity the length of the hair changes by 2½ per cent. To make the device more rugged, several hairs (or a piece of ox gut) can be used. A lever magnifies the movement that can be read on a scale. If you let the lever work a pen, and provide a revolving drum, you can make a permanent record of the changing humidity of the air.

Around 1800 another instrument was designed to measure the moisture in the air. It's the most accurate in use today. It is made of two thermometers mounted side by side. The bulb of one thermometer is covered by a wet cotton wick. You whirl the whole apparatus by a string looped at the end—hence the name sling-psychrometer—or by a swiveled handle to create good air circulation. Or you turn on an electric fan in the standard thermometer shelter.

The dry-bulb thermometer indicates the air temperature. The wet-bulb thermometer, cooled by evaporation, will read a lower temperature. To get proper evaporation you have to whirl the psychrometer quite rapidly and keep up the effort until the wet-bulb thermometer doesn't go down any farther. (The stationary gadget you see on an executive's desk doesn't work properly.)

When the humidity of the air is so high that no amount of whirling causes evaporation, both thermometers will read the same temperature. That's the condition that leads to formation of dew. Hence the temperature—now indicated by both thermometers—is called the *dew point* temperature, or simply the dew point.

Most of the time you'll get two different readings on the two thermometers. When it's very humid the difference between the two temperatures will be small; when in air of the same temperature the humidity is lower, the spread between readings will be larger.

With the psychrometer come tables in which you can find the moisture content of the air. In the same tables you can also find the present dew point. That is the temperature at which the air you have just measured would form dew, or—if other conditions are right—fog.

The most familiar measure of humidity of the air is *relative* humidity. The usual definition—percentage of water air of a given temperature can hold—is not quite accurate, but it will do. Air at its dew point temperature, saturated air, has a relative humidity of 100 per cent. Air from which all water vapor has been removed, has a relative humidity of 0 per cent at any temperature.

In between these extremes the relative humidity varies with the "capacity of air to hold moisture." And that depends on the temperature of the air. It about doubles for a rise in temperature of 20 degrees Fahrenheit (10 degrees Celsius).

Take an example. One cool and delightful morning you get up early. There's dew on the grass: the relative humidity is near 100 per cent, the temperature about 60° F (15° C). At noon the temperature stands at about 78° F (25° C). The moisture content of the air hasn't changed at all, but now the relative humidity stands at 50 per cent.

To avoid this difficulty you could specify how many grains of water are contained in a pound of air at a given moment. That would show that in the above example no change has taken place.

And how could you weigh that? That's simple. Just look on a different page of your psychrometric tables.

Meteorologists routinely use such a measure. But they express it in internationally agreed units: so many grams of water in one kilogram of air. Actually they use two units. One, the specific humidity, gives grams of water in a kilogram of air as it is. The other, the mixing ratio, measures grams of water in one kilogram of *dry* air, that is the weight of air after the water content has been subtracted. Since the mass of water is only a very small percentage of the mass of air, the two calculations give virtually the same figures.

At some weather stations the dew point is automatically recorded. The apparatus is ingenious. A light shines on a metal mirror that reflects it onto a photoelectric cell. The mirror is then cooled. When beads of dew form, the light reaching the cell drops sharply. That makes it transmit the temperature of the mirror to a recorder inside the office. The cooling stops temporarily, only to be restarted after a set lapse of time.

You probably neither need nor want such an instrument. But almost everyone sooner or later suffers under some combination of temperature and humidity. We all know that dry cold is more tolerable than wet, that dry heat is less aggravating than the same temperature when it's muggy, humid.

Measuring these conditions runs into a problem: Different people react very differently. So experimenters trying to establish a Discomfort Index took many subjects, and submitted them to varying combinations of temperature and humidity. Then they noted the point where a few people began to feel uncomfortable, where half the people would complain, and where almost everybody would quit, if he could.

But agreement on what's most comfortable is not universal. Example: In the United States, air-conditioning engineers aim at 72° F (22° C) with a relative humidity of 40–60 per cent. Their British counterparts design for 65° F (18° C) and a 50–60 per cent relative humidity.

Either set of figures, by the way, shows that it is not enough to cool the air—except in desert country. Say the outside temperature is 90° F (32° C), the relative humidity 50 per cent. By the time you cooled a cinema to 72° F (22° C), fog would form. Everybody would complain. If you cooled it to 65° F (18° C), rain would fall on the patrons who had not yet walked out. To prevent bankruptcy you would also have to extract some water from the air.

Quite a lot of water. In the room we used to calculate the weight of air you'd have to get rid of 1½ pints (0.75 l) every time the air changed. That's without anyone in the room adding water by breathing and by imperceptible perspiration. No wonder you get dripped on when you pass under some window air-conditioners.

Dehumidified to 50 per cent relative humidity, the room that contains about a man's weight of air will still contain about 1½ pounds (0.75 kg) of water vapor.

There must then be a lot of water suspended in the world's atmosphere. Judge for yourself. If you condensed all of it, you'd get a layer about 2 inches (5 cm) deep in the tropics, and just a trace over the polar regions. Averaged over the entire world, you'd get about one inch (2.5 cm). Seven tenths of that would condense over the oceans, and the rest would soon get there. The sea level, worldwide, would rise about 1¼ inches (3.25 cm). That's all.

That is surprising for another reason. The worldwide rainfall in one year is estimated to average about 35 inches (90 cm). That's about thirty-five times the total water content of the atmosphere of earth. So the entire stock of moisture must be turned over that many times a year, about once every ten days.

Such efficiency must be the envy of every merchant. Especially when you think how far some of the merchandise has to be freighted. The water in the rain or snow that falls on Boston may have come from the Gulf of Mexico or perhaps the Pacific.

You have read about measuring wind direction and speed, air temperature, barometric pressure, and humidity. You can see how these concepts will be needed later to explain winds.

But you may wonder what other instruments are used in observing the weather. Put differently: If you wanted to have a complete weather station, what instruments would you need besides the ones discussed?

Only one. Some gadget to measure precipitation.

Rainfall has been recorded for a long time. We have figures from India and Palestine from before the birth of Christ. All you need is a container and some way to measure the quantity of water collected.

There are difficulties. On many days your bucket would collect only a small fraction of one inch, or even of a centimeter. And if you wait overnight, or twenty-four hours—not to mention a week or a month—a good part of the water in the bucket will have evaporated before you measure it.

One solution: Catch the rain over a larger area than the one you measure. You could let a large funnel drain into a small graduate. If the diameter of the funnel is ten times that of the graduate, you'll get one inch of water in your beaker for every hundredth of an inch of rain. The smaller surface will also reduce the evaporation.

A rain gauge can be made to make a permanent record by putting it on a scale. A suitable linkage drives a pen that leaves a trace on the usual clock-driven drum. Between rains that line should be horizontal. Any drop in weight is obviously due to evaporation.

The weather bureau also uses a device called a tipping-bucket rain gauge, said to have been invented by Sir Christopher Wren, better known as the architect of much of London after the fire of 1666. When the thimble-size bucket is full, it upsets, empties itself, and operates a counter. If 0.01 inch of rain over the funnel fills the bucket, twenty tippings will mean 0.20 inch of rain has fallen. The counter is easily wired to record inside the building.

Snow and hail pose small problems. Both can be melted and recorded as water equivalent. Snowfall can also be measured in inches (or centimeters) by poking an ordinary ruler straight into it. The trick is to find spots where the wind hasn't either heaped it up or blown some of it away. Often snowfall is converted into water using the formula ten inches of freshly fallen (wet) snow equals one inch of rain.

Most other observations of the weather are made with the eyes only. Visibility for instance can be recorded as the most distant object clearly visible. When you can just make out a TV tower three miles away, you log visibility three miles. Other objects could be the end of a runway, the wind sock, landing lights on an airport. . . .

Yes, there is an electric device that measures the weakening of a light in a sample of air, but you don't need that. Just find yourself some prominent objects and get their distance from you from a map of your town.

Your eyes, and the instructions for weather observers, will tell you the "total amount of cloud" (5/10 means the sky is half covered) and the type of low, middle, and high clouds present (match clouds with pictures).

And so for most of the other observations.

When you are interested in the *climate* of a place, you may want to know the hours of sunshine there. It isn't practical to have someone with a stopwatch sit around every day from sunrise to sunset and keep a record.

It can be done with a gadget I have admired since as a boy I learned to burn a hole in a piece of paper with a lens. The sunshine meter is a glass sphere under which there is a piece of ruled paper. When the sun shines, it burns a string of holes which appear as a solid scorched line. The rate of the angular movement of the sun—or if you prefer, of the earth—is the same all year long and everywhere. So it is easy to translate the length of the scorch marks into hours and fractions.

This beautifully simple device has been replaced with a *sunshine duration transmitter*. Its heart is a blackened tube filled with mercury. When the sun shines, the tube gets hot, and the mercury expands and closes an electric contact that—you guessed it—operates a pen on a revolving drum somewhere inside the office.

Or you can cut out the mercury business and use photo cells in a sunshine switch.

7

Local Winds and Monsoons

It'd be nice if I could report that the invention of the instruments that measure temperature, air pressure, and humidity brought a general understanding of the processes in the atmosphere. If that had been so, I could now lay out before you the progress made, and thereby explain the winds and the weather.

But let's look at the record.

Almost two centuries after Leonardo da Vinci's discovery of a method for measuring moisture in the air, more than one century after the invention of thermometer and barometer, the *Encyclopaedia Britannica* in its first edition (1771) explains why the barometer is lowest in violent storms: The wind moves so fast horizontally that it doesn't press down much vertically. And when does rain and snow fall? When the air is too light and thin, as shown by the low barometer, to bear the vapors. In fair weather the air is too dense and heavy, as shown by the high barometer, to let them fall.

Pure Aristotle in modern dress.

But great progress toward a weather science had been made. Newton had sorted out the concepts of mass, force, and gravity. Of more direct interest, the basic gas law had been discovered. If you went to school in an English-speaking country, you learned it as Boyle's law. In France you would have called it Mariotte's law. In Austria, where I first heard about it, it was Boyle-Mariotte's law.

By whatever name, you have probably forgotten the formula that connects volume, pressure, and temperature of a gas. But you know many of its consequences. Warm air is less dense, lighter, than cold air. Compressing air warms it; that's why the bicycle pump gets hot. When a gas expands, it cools; that's why frost forms on the nozzle when you release air from a scuba tank, or carbon dioxide from a fire extinguisher.

With only such well-known, homely laws you can explain a number of local winds and some not so local winds.

Imagine an island in a tropical sea. After sunrise the land warms. The air above the land becomes less dense than the air all around it, and rises. Cool air from the ocean gets pulled in to feed the updraft. Or you could say the higher pressure over the cooler ocean pushes the air in. You could get even more scientific. The result is the same: a sea breeze that starts in the morning, and increases until the warmest time of the day, the afternoon.

That breeze will taper off and die down around sunset. At night the situation is reversed. The sea stays warm, while the land cools. The cooler, heavier land air will drain toward the ocean as a land breeze.

Along the coast of a continent and some miles inland the situation is similar. Land and sea breezes will blow roughly at right angles to the coastline.

In the tropics these land and sea breezes are superimposed on the large-scale winds, now reinforcing, now weakening them. Where the general air flow is from the east, a sea breeze will strengthen the wind on the eastern shore, where the two work together. It will weaken the wind on the western shore, where the sea breeze blows against the general air flow.

In the temperate zones the large-scale winds at times may totally hide the effect of the local land and sea breezes.

In mountainous country regular winds are often caused by locally uneven heating just as in the sea and land breezes. In the afternoon, rising warmer air flows up the valley floor and up the side slopes. During the night, cold air pours down the slopes and down the valley.

In a valley that opens to the ocean, afternoon sea breeze and up-valley drafts combine. The sea air may be almost saturated with moisture. A small drop in temperature at sunset then fills the entire valley with fog.

So far I have only talked about strictly local heating and cooling, the difference between day and night. But the same mechanism can explain some *seasonal,* far from local winds—winds that blow in summer from ocean to heated continent, in winter from continental cold areas toward the warmer sea. The best-known example: the monsoons of India. To this day sailing vessels, as they have done since antiquity, use them to cross the Arabian Sea to India in summer and to make the return trip in winter.

Our simple observation that cold air is denser, heavier, than warm air explains some chilly winds. Examples: the fierce *mistral* that funnels down the Rhone valley, the *bora* that rushes down to the coast of the Adriatic. These and similar descending winds, technically known as fall winds, are simply cold air pulled by gravity, like water in a waterfall.

You may have a doubt. The air in these winds, descending to sea level and increasing air pressure, gets compressed. Doesn't that warm it? It does. But the air is so cold to start with, that it still makes the French Riviera feel like a ski resort.

But what of *warm* downslope winds, the *chinook* of the eastern Rockies, the *foehn* of the Alps, the *Santa Ana* of southern California? For that matter, "the warm winds from cold regions" that had already puzzled Theophrastus.

To explain their warmth we need two other homely principles.

ONE: It takes heat to turn water into steam. You knew that. But did you know that it takes six and a half times as much energy to turn a quantity of water to steam as it took to heat it from room temperature to boiling? (That's why I still have some pots. If it takes five minutes for a kettle to come to the boil, I have more than a half hour before it boils dry.)

TWO: Energy is indestructible. It can change form, but it's still around somewhere. The water vapor, so costly in energy to produce, carries that energy with it. That invisible energy is technically known as the latent heat of evaporation. That latent heat shows up again as ordinary heat when water vapor turns back to liquid form.

That liberated latent heat is what makes the foehn and similar winds warm. Imagine a parcel of air containing no moisture at all crossing the Alps or the Rockies. It would cool on climbing—

because it expands—and then would warm at the same rate in coming down on the other side—because it is compressed by the greater atmospheric pressure. Result: The parcel of air would have the same temperature at the same elevation on either side of the mountains.

Now follow another parcel of air across the Rockies. It has come recently from the Pacific and is laden with moisture. As it climbs, it again cools. Soon its temperature reaches the dew point. Clouds form. Higher up it rains. By the time the air parcel reaches the crest of the mountains, all its water vapor has returned to the liquid state. And all the sun's energy that originally evaporated the water over the Pacific Ocean is liberated, and heats the now-dry air parcel. That's quite apart from the heating by compression as the air descends. Result: At the same elevation the air parcel is considerably warmer on the far side of the mountains.

The warming can be spectacular. In midwinter in Calgary, at the eastern base of the Canadian Rockies, I have seen a foot of snow melt in one hour. Buds opened, the trees mistaking the chinook for spring. No wonder. It had been 25° F (−4° C); fifteen minutes later, the thermometer stood at 61° F (16° C).

Simple concepts also explain the winds around local thunderstorms, the kind most common in summer in the afternoon. (I'll talk later about other thunderstorms—connected with traveling weather—that occur in all seasons and at any time of day.)

In simplest terms the local thunderstorm forms from massive updrafts of locally warmed air. The winds around it resemble the sea breezes around a warmed island: Air streams in from all sides to replace the rising air.

That has fooled many a sailor. He sees a thundercloud growing and feels the wind that blows *toward* the build-up. "That one can't hurt us; it's downwind of us."

But soon, when rain and perhaps hail begin to fall, there is a sudden rush of air *downward*. As that air hits the water, it fans out in all directions. Our sailor, if he didn't get all sail off her at the first breath of cold air, may be in trouble.

That explanation, admittedly simplified, is clear enough. But you may wonder why not every updraft starts thunderstorms.

A small updraft, from air warmed over a clearing in a forest, a sandspit in a lake, a paved parking lot at a golf course . . . , hasn't got a chance. As it rises, it will mix around the edges with the air through which it travels, and cool before it has risen very far.

Only several rising columns of air, close together, will survive this "entrainment" of cold air. You can actually see the individual columns, or cells, in a building thundercloud. They look—if you'll pardon the mixed metaphor—like towering cauliflower, bunched together.

8

Trade Winds and Doldrums

Can the simple gas laws explain not only local winds—and monsoons—but the large-scale winds all over the world?

Let's first look at one half of the world, the area between 30° N
and 30° S latitude. It doesn't sound like half the world. And on
the usual maps, which inflate Greenland to the size of Africa, it
doesn't look like half. But it is. You can check it on a globe.

More than three fourths of that half of the globe is oceans.
Over most of them blow year-round easterly winds: the northeast
trade winds in the northern hemisphere, the southeast trade winds
in the southern.

The name trade winds or trades, according to language experts,
has nothing to do with commerce, although for several centuries
they pushed cargoes over vast stretches of ocean. Instead, we are
told, the name comes from an obsolete meaning of trade, related
to track and tread. And indeed for days and sometimes weeks on
end these winds follow the same track. There is yet another meaning of trade: regular course of action. The trades certainly are the
most regular of all winds. Over most of the ocean area under dis-
cussion you'd be right 80 per cent of the time if you predicted
wind direction *and* wind speed from a climate chart for that
month.

You may recall the trouble they caused Columbus. After sailing
day after day before the easterly breeze, even the densest sailor in
his crew could figure out that they'd never be able to get back to
Spain.

Columbus and the navigators that followed him reported

masses of floating sargassum weed. So the first explanation for the recently experienced trade winds was simple: The trades are the exhalation of the sargassum weed.

The explanation given almost three hundred years later in the *Encyclopaedia Britannica* is not much better:

> And here we must observe that as the point upon which the sun acts with the greatest power is constantly moving from east to west, the air to the east of that point over which the sun has more lately passed will be more rarified than to the west, and will naturally flow toward that point from east to west with greater velocity than from west to east, as the cool air to the west of that point will be interrupted in its motion towards it by the motion of the sun meeting it.
>
> Hence therefore it follows, that from the diurnal motion of the earth from west to east a constant east wind would always be produced, were it not obstructed by other causes.
>
> But as there is a constant stream of air flowing from the polar towards the equatorial regions, a composition of these two currents of air acting at the same time will produce a north-east wind in *all* parts of the northern hemisphere, and a south-east wind in *all* parts of the southern one.
>
> These winds are known by the name of *the general trade-winds*.

(To make this rarefied prose a bit more readable I have taken the liberty of making sentences into paragraphs and emphasizing —twice—the word *all*.)

The anonymous author has explained that wind that replaces the air near the equator which has risen due to greater warming combines with east wind caused by the westward movement of the sun during the day. That, he says, causes northeast winds all over the northern hemisphere, southeast winds all over the southern. Having explained these general trade winds, he erases most of them:

In all those regions towards the poles, as the influence of the sun is there but weak, other lesser causes occasion particular winds, and disturb that regularity which at first view we might expect, so that the *general trade wind* does not invariably take place beyond the 28th or 30th degree of latitude; and the regions between that and the poles have nothing but variable winds.

Even in the Torrid Zone, there are many causes which in particular places alter this direction of the wind; so that the *genuine trade-winds* do not take place except in the Atlantic and Pacific oceans on each side of the equator to the distance of 28 or 30 degrees, and in the greatest part of the Indian ocean to the south of the Equator.

The torrid zone is the area I was talking about; the *genuine* trade winds are the ones we are interested in. And the limits given in the last paragraph are about right, although they vary with the seasons. In the northern Indian Ocean they are masked by the monsoons discussed in the preceding chapter.

Here is the modern explanation of the trade winds. The air that (on a nonrevolving earth) flows toward the equator does not come from the poles. It starts from the horse latitudes, areas of calms and usually clear skies just poleward of the trade wind belts. There the air that has risen nearer the equator comes down again to the surface. From there it would flow toward the equator to replace the rising air.

On an earth that did not revolve, that would cause a north wind on the surface in the northern hemisphere (and a south wind aloft). And a south wind on the surface in the southern hemisphere (and a north wind aloft).

But the earth does revolve. That motion makes the equator-bound winds in both hemispheres seem to come from a more easterly direction. An observer rotating with the surface of the earth will log northeasterly winds in the northern hemisphere, southeasterly winds in the southern.

I'll spare you the mathematical details. But this "modern" explanation had been given already by Hadley a generation before the *Britannica* was published.

The actually observed trade winds near the surface, averaged over large areas and the whole year, show wind speeds of 12–20 knots in the east-west direction, 2–4 knots in the direction of the equator.

They are delightful winds. In thousands of observations you'll find always several degrees difference between the dry-bulb and the wet-bulb temperatures. More practically: As long as you stay in the breeze it will dry your skin—or your shirt, if you wear a shirt—before it even gets moist. That accounts for the year-round popularity of resorts on the windward side of tropical islands.

If you want to take photographs, you'll have puffy cotton-ball clouds for background almost always. They are such a fixture that textbooks call them *trade wind cumulus*. Like all cumulus clouds, they are caused by updrafts of warm air in which the water vapor begins to condense when it reaches the level where the atmosphere is at the dew-point temperature.

But these cumulus clouds normally don't grow into towering thunderheads. The reason: a temperature inversion. We all know that the temperature drops as you go higher. But in the trade wind belts there is almost everywhere, almost all the time, a layer of air that's warmer than the air directly below it. That keeps a lid on the updrafts.

In a modern sailboat you don't have to go downwind. You can trim your sails and lash your wheel, hour after hour, certain that the wind will get you where you want to go . . . the next island, or—westabout—around the world.

I have lived and sailed in the trade wind belt for several years, and lived on its fringes many more years. But I have never battled the doldrums, the zone between the northeast and southeast trades. At times that zone—the intertropical convergence zone, or ITC, is its official name—has no width at all. At other times and other places, it may stretch over 8 degrees of latitude, about 500 nautical miles (900 km). The zone moves seasonally north and south with the sun, but almost always stays just north of the geographic equator.

Listen to what it's like from people who should know, small-craft sailors. First, Captain Joshua Slocum, the first solo circum-navigator of the earth, in *Spray*, about 40 feet (12 m) on deck:

> On the following day [September 15, 1895, between the Cape Verde Islands and South America] heavy rain clouds rose to the south, obscuring the sun; this was ominous of doldrums. On the 16th *Spray* entered this gloomy region, to battle with squalls and to be harassed by fitful calms; for this is the state of the elements between the northeast and southeast trades, where each wind, struggling in turn for mastery, expends its force whirling about in all directions. Making this still more trying to one's nerve and patience, the sea was tossed into confused lumps and fretted by eddying currents. As if something more were needed to complete a sailor's discomfort in this state, the rain poured down in torrents day and night. The *Spray* struggled and tossed for ten days, making only three hundred miles on her course in all that time.

Captain J. C. Voss in 1901 set out to circumnavigate the world to help win a bet that it could be done in a craft smaller than Slocum's. The man who put up the money for the voyage and was to travel with Voss must have had quite a shock when he saw the craft: an aging Indian canoe, hollowed out from a cedar log, 5½ feet (1.7 m) wide, and 30 feet (9 m) on the bottom. Voss strengthened the hull, raised the topsides, added a keel, decked her, rigged three (!) masts, and added a cabin with sitting headroom and only large enough for one bunk.

About 1,500 miles west of Acapulco, Mexico, he reports:

> In the latter part of July, when in latitude seventeen degrees north and longitude one hundred and twenty-five west, the trade wind became light, and the sky cloudy. At three o'clock in the afternoon a heavy westerly squall, accompanied by rain struck *Tilikum*, which made us take in sail pretty quickly. The squall was short and sweet, but I knew then, by the way the weather acted,

that we had sailed out of the north-east trade wind and got into what is called the calm belt or Doldrums.

It is rather unusual, and certainly very unlucky, to lose the north-east trade wind as soon as that, as it generally means a long spell of dirty weather, which we certainly got. Why that part of the ocean is called the calm belt I don't understand, because, from the trouble we had with *Tilikum,* and also from former experiences, I should call it anything but that. "The belt of seamen's trouble" would be a far more suitable name.

For sixteen long days and nights we had nothing but trouble with the weather and the sails; it was up sails and down sails, hauling in sheets or slacking them, all the time. During that time, we experienced about fifty changes of weather every day. It would be pouring with rain for a little while, and then the sun would blaze down on us. The next thing would be a heavy squall of wind and rain combined, but my mate and I stuck to it. . . .

On the return trip—between Pernambuco and the Azores— Voss had to cross the doldrums again. Would it be another fortnight of misery?

The North Atlantic calm belt did not turn out as troublesome as its counterpart in the Pacific three years previously. After two days of variable weather, spells of calms interspersed with puffs of air from different directions and accompanied by rain showers, we passed into the influence of the north-east trade winds.

The books of other small-craft circumnavigators are full of woes in the doldrums.

The three-man crew of *Ho-Ho*, a Norwegian cutter, 39 feet (12 m) long reports:

For eight days since we lost contact with the northeast trade wind until we found the south-east wind, our average distance had been under twenty miles a day. If we had *walked* the distance, at an even pace day and night, we could have covered it in half the time.

Some aren't even that lucky. Alain Gerbault, a Frenchman, batted about west of Panama in *Firecrest* from June 17 to July 2, 1925. Her position on that last day was only five miles south of the one plotted seventeen days earlier.

Sir Francis Chichester, who, sixty-five years old, singlehanded the racing machine *Gipsy Moth IV* the hard way around the world—from England, by way of the Cape of Good Hope, Australia, and Cape Horn—summed up all sailors' feelings about the doldrums in his log entry for April 25, 1967: "To hell with the whole outfit!"

9

What Drives
the Global Winds?

Local differences in temperature explain local winds. The same
differences on larger scale account for the monsoons. Add the
effect of the rotation of earth, and you have a mechanism that
drives the trade winds in both hemispheres. Let these trade winds
collide and you have an explanation of sorts for the doldrums.

But there simply are no general trade winds, as the earliest Britannica wants us to believe. We can't use an explanation like the
one Hadley used for the winds of the two temperate zones. That
would only lead to an airflow from some easterly direction. And in
these zones, in both hemispheres, the prevailing winds are *not*
easterly. On the contrary, in these areas, where by the way most of
the world's population lives, *westerly* circulation predominates.
That circulation is often interrupted by short-term winds from all
other directions.

When you come to think of it, prevailing westerlies over large
areas of the globe are necessary.

Easterly winds blow against the rotation of the earth. Friction
at the surface would slow that rotation. With the trades blowing
year in and year out over half the surface of the globe, that effect
should become noticeable. The days should become longer. But
they don't. (What little slowing has been measured by astronomers is fully accounted for by other influences, mainly the tides.)

Therefore, as Aristotle may have reasoned, westerly winds in higher latitudes must in the long run balance the retarding effect of the trade winds.

What drives these winds? Again the answer is heat. The only significant source of that heat is the sun. Other sources—heat seeping from the interior of the earth directly or in hot springs and volcanoes, radioactivity, burning of fossil fuels, the heat given off by animals and plants—all are totally negligible by comparison with the heat earth receives from the sun.

The earth is at an annual mean distance of about 93 million statute miles (150 million km) from the sun. At that distance 1.35 kilowatts of solar energy fall on every square meter. That important figure, the solar constant, doesn't mean much even if you know that a square meter is a square of about 39 inches (somewhat larger than a folding card table).

If you set up a 100 per cent efficient solar panel of that size and kept it always turned toward the sun, you could make about 4 cents worth of electricity every hour (at a rate of 3 cents per kwh). One hundred such bridge-table-size panels, say on a spacecraft, would generate $4.00 worth of electricity in one hour.

You probably don't own a spacecraft. If you did, how would you get the electricity to where you can use or sell it—the surface of earth? So you had better set up your panels on earth.

Before you get carried away and calculate how many kilowatts or dollars you could make by covering the whole earth with such panels, remember an important fact. The earth is a sphere. And it turns on its axis. On the average, your earth-mounted panels would yield only one-fourth the output of panels carried by a spacecraft and always facing the sun. The output is down to $1.00 per 100 square meters.

We still have to refine our calculation. Your energy-collecting panels are not set up in space, but at the bottom of earth's atmosphere. And funny things happen to solar energy on the way through the atmosphere. Some is absorbed; even more gets reflected right back into space, mostly by the tops of clouds.

(Astronomers had found a clever way of measuring that reflected light before we had spacecraft or even high-flying planes. They measured the light reflected from earth onto the moon.

That "ashen light," especially noticeable a day or two after new moon as "the old moon in the arms of the new," gave a figure in close agreement with measurements made from spacecraft.)

Everybody now agrees that your dollar's worth of energy at the top of the atmosphere has shrunk to about 47 cents when it reaches the earth's surface.

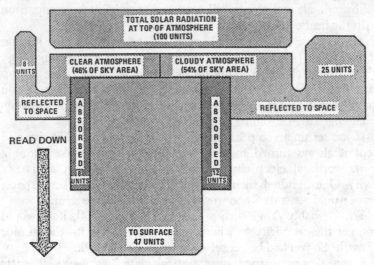

TOTAL SOLAR RADIATION
AT TOP OF ATMOSPHERE
(100 UNITS)

8 UNITS

CLEAR ATMOSPHERE
(46% OF SKY AREA)

CLOUDY ATMOSPHERE
(54% OF SKY AREA)

25 UNITS

REFLECTED TO SPACE

ABSORBED
8 UNITS

ABSORBED
12 UNITS

REFLECTED TO SPACE

READ DOWN

TO SURFACE
47 UNITS

8. Solar radiation and atmosphere

That's still a lot of power. Enough for one oversized card table to run a 150-watt light bulb constantly. Is that the power that drives the winds?

Far from it. All that energy is returned to the atmosphere and to space. This has to be so. If the earth's surface retained ever so little of the radiation received, the land, lakes, rivers, and oceans would get warmer all the time. Now the average annual temperature of the world's surface is about 60° F (15° C). It has been very close to that temperature for hundreds of years. (We know that for the time before thermometers from the limits of sensitive crops. We know, for instance, where the Romans grew grapes, and where Italy's climate was too rugged for vineyards.)

The radiation from the sun reaches the surface of earth in the form of light, heat, and some ultraviolet radiation that gives you a tan. It is all returned from the surface as heat, or if you want a fancier term, as infrared radiation. But energy is energy. We can calculate the reflected heat in the same units as the radiation received. Just as your friendly power company charges you in kilowatt-hours for its product derived from heat (coal, oil, or nuclear reactions) or gravity acting on water. And just as they charge in kilowatt-hours whether you use the electricity to light your house, heat your water, or roast a duck in your microwave oven.

At our agreed rate of 3 cents per kwh, you'd expect the surface to give up as much as it received—on the average 47 cents for an area covered by one hundred oversized card tables. Surprisingly that 100-square-meter area radiates 61 cents' worth of energy. You'd think the world would soon be covered by ice all over. But the budget deficit is only apparent: The clouds reflect 14 cents' worth back to earth.

So the budget is in balance. The overall temperature of the globe will remain constant. There is a simple mechanism built into the atmosphere that acts as a thermostat for the earth surface.

Suppose the world should warm up for some reason. That would increase evaporation; more clouds would form. The added cloud cover would cut down the sunshine reaching the ground. It would get cooler.

On the other hand, should the surface cool down for some reason, evaporation would be less, clouds fewer. Sunshine would increase, and the surface would get warmer.

There is another, more sophisticated thermostat. According to a well-proven physical law, the amount of energy radiated away increases with rising temperature. (That's why your coffee will cool quicker if you don't add the cream until later.) Should the surface of our globe warm, it would lose more heat than now. It would cool until outgoing and incoming energy would again balance.

Now take the opposite case. If the surface cooled, it would lose less heat than now until the balance was restored.

What happens to all the heat lost by the surface? The greatest

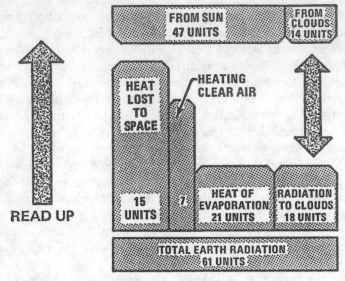

9. Radiation balance of earth

part is used in evaporating water, making clouds. Some escapes to space, some heats the air directly. And a lot, as you have already seen, goes up to the clouds, which return a good part of it.

That last effect explains, by the way, why the ground cools so much more on a cloudless night. There are no clouds to return the loss.

Here is an important fact: The atmosphere—cloudy and clear combined—lets through 47 cents' worth of radiation from the sun. It lets only 32 cents' worth of the radiation from earth pass into space. Reason: Though fairly transparent to *light*, gases in the atmosphere—mainly water vapor and carbon dioxide—strongly absorb infrared radiation, that is heat.

As a result, the surface is kept at a higher average temperature than it would be without these gases. That has been called the *greenhouse effect*. The idea. The world is made livable for us, just as we assure the survival of plants in a northern winter by placing them in a greenhouse. The explanation: Solar radiation —17 cents' worth even on an overcast day—is trapped by the glass, which does not let infrared radiation escape. Then someone spoiled that nice simile. He replaced the glass in a greenhouse with sheets of rock salt, which is transparent to infrared radiation. The temperature was about the same.

Now I don't want to leave you with the idea that the atmosphere as a whole keeps squirreling away heat. It can't. It too must have a balanced heat budget or it would get warmer all the time. It obviously doesn't.

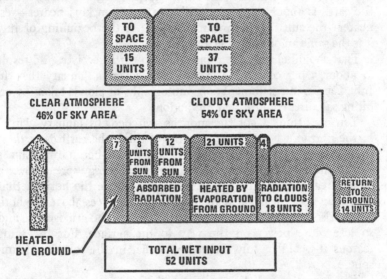

10. Radiation balance in atmosphere

If you study the heat budget of the atmosphere, you'll find that it receives only 20 cents' worth of energy from the sun, while it gets 32 cents net from the earth. This heating from below helps to explain the well-known fact that the air gets cooler the higher you go (at least in the first few miles or kilometers).

All these figures, though subject to argument about a cent or so, are as reliable as you could hope. Some admit indirect checks. They must, for instance, yield the known global mean temperature. And the worldwide evaporation must be balanced by the estimated precipitation over the whole globe. The surprisingly small stock of water in the atmosphere would soon be exhausted if more rain fell than evaporated. If less, rain clouds would soon cover all the world.

There is also a rather elegant "experimental" check on the figures. The solar constant, the basis of all the calculations, is calculated for the *mean* distance of the earth from the sun, 93 million statute miles (150 million km). But the orbit of earth around the sun is not a circle but an ellipse. At the beginning of January the earth is about 1.6 million miles (2.5 million km) nearer—yes, nearer—the sun than its mean distance. At the beginning of July it is the same amount farther away.

That should change the total radiation earth receives, and result in about 5 per cent more overall cloudcover in January than in July. Careful measurements on photographs of clouds taken by orbiting satellites confirm that prediction.

You may think I got the months switched. In January, winter in the northern hemisphere, you might think the earth is *farthest* from the sun. Not so. It's cold there in winter because the sun is low in the sky and a given amount of solar energy spreads over a larger area. (When the sun is 45 degrees above the horizon that area is 22 per cent larger than when it is 60 degrees above the horizon.) Also its rays have a longer path through the atmosphere and so lose more power on the way to the surface. For the same reasons it's cold in July, in say Australia, in the southern hemisphere.

The figures of radiation received and heat lost have referred to the earth's surface as a whole, and the atmosphere as a whole. Obviously there will be areas where you'll get—or lose—more than the mean radiation. You'll do better setting up your solar panels in the tropics than near the poles. Just as you'd do better with a banana plantation in the West Indies than in Saskatchewan.

Geometry lets us calculate the radiation received in any latitude, for any hour of any day of the year. Another calculation lets us estimate the heat lost there. The angle of the sun in any one latitude changes with the time of day and the date. The length of the period between sunrise and sunset changes with date and latitude, from eleven to thirteen hours in the tropics, up to six months at the poles. That leads to a paradox: In midsummer the North Pole gets more sunshine than a point on the equator—simply because the day is about twice as long.

Averaged over the year *one* square meter of horizontal surface receives in one day 20 cents' worth of solar energy on the equator, 4 cents' worth at the North Pole.

On the equator and all through the tropics the ground and the air above it gain 3 cents' worth per day more than they lose. In high latitudes they lose more than they receive. At the poles the net average loss is 9 cents' worth a day.

Somewhere in between there must be a strip where income and outgo of energy just balance. In the northern hemisphere the break-even point is near latitude 38° N. That's about the latitude of San Francisco, Washington, D.C., or Lisbon.

Let's see if we can use this surplus of energy in one area and the deficit in another to explain the winds on a global scale.

For that, imagine an experiment that any high-school physics lab could set up at minimal cost. The main piece of apparatus is a flat-bottomed metal pan that can be made to rotate around its center at different speeds. The pan represents one hemisphere of the earth, the rim the equator, the pan's center one of the poles. Now pour some water into the pan to simulate the lower atmosphere. Something is needed to make the circulation visible. Aluminum powder has been used in the experiment, originally suggested by Dave Fultz of the University of Chicago; sawdust works too.

To simulate the excess heat near the equator, arrange some way of heating the pan at the rim. To simulate the net heat loss at the polar regions, arrange for cooling at the center.

Now the experiment, universally called the "dishpan" experiment, can begin. At first the pan stands still. You'll get just about what you'd expect: Near the rim heated water will rise, near the center it will sink. You'll get warmed water on top flowing toward the center, sinking and returning along the bottom of the pan. (This *overturning* circulation probably reminds you of the process in the atmosphere between the equator and the horse latitudes.)

Next we set the pan revolving to simulate the rotation of the

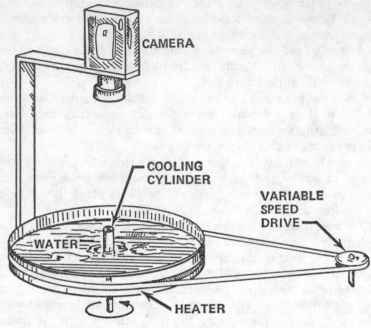

11. Dishpan experiment

earth. We are interested in the circulation as seen from the carrousel itself, not by someone watching it from a distance. So we mount a movie camera directly over the pan and revolving with it.

When the pan revolves slowly, say at one revolution per minute, a new pattern appears. Suppose the pan rotates counterclockwise as seen from above. That would simulate the northern hemisphere seen from above the North Pole.

Follow a single particle floating on top of the water. It will still move from rim to center as before. But at the same time it will also drift to the right as it gets farther from the rim. Explanation: Near the rim the particle acquires a certain momentum from the rotation of the pan. (Just as you acquire momentum traveling on a bus; if you jump off before the bus stops, you carry that momentum with you and go splat on the sidewalk.) As that particle gets closer to the center of the pan, it still carries the momentum acquired at the rim. If the pan is 10 inches (25 cm) across and turns at one revolution per minute, a particle near the rim will have a speed of about 30 inches (75 cm) per minute. Halfway to the center it will still have this speed. But here a point on the bottom of the pan turns at only half that rate. The particle—besides moving toward the center—will be moving to the right at a speed of 15 inches (37 cm) per minute in relation to the bottom. In the film the tracks of individual particles will not be straight lines from rim to center but spirals.

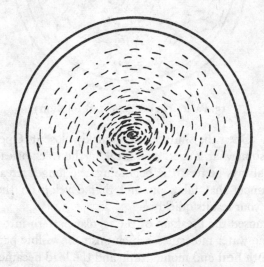

12. Pattern in dishpan (slow rotation)

Worse confusion is to come. Increase the rate of rotation of the pan to, say, 5 rpm. You'll see the entire neat pattern break up before your eyes. You'll see meandering waves, whirls, and eddies. The developed film will show that some of these whirls turn clockwise, some counterclockwise.

(You could mount a still camera rather than a movie camera to rotate with the pan. On a short time-exposure you'd see a general blur indicating the pattern of motion. But you couldn't tell in which direction the vortices whirled. Here is a trick: Set the shut-

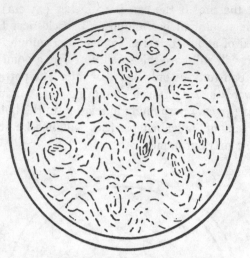

13. Pattern in dishpan (fast rotation)

ter on "B." Open the shutter, then quickly close it. Open it again, this time somewhat longer. The break in the track of each particle will then always be near the beginning, the longer streak near the end. A camera that takes pictures that develop on the spot lets you check your results quickly.)

What caused the break-up of the regular pattern into waves and whirls? The water molecules, which push the visible particles, had to carry both heat and momentum, and the load became too heavy to make the entire trip from rim to center. The new set-up is more efficient. Waves and whirls transport heat and momentum—from rim to center—without moving far from the zone where their inherent speed is the speed of the bottom of the pan.

The appearance of the circulation in the rotating dishpan strikingly resembles a weather map of the northern hemisphere. (See figure 38, near the very end of the book.)

But water is not air, a flat pan not a sphere. Are the conditions in the earth's atmosphere similar? Imagine a parcel of air at rest over the northern Gulf of Mexico moving north to transfer excess heat to colder regions. In latitude 30° N, near New Orleans, any

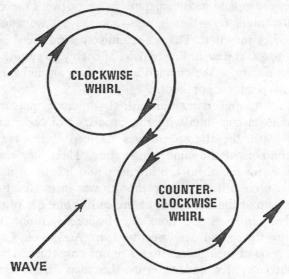

14. Whirls and waves in the dishpan, without moving themselves from rim to center, even out temperature differences between heated and cooled areas.

The clockwise whirl, on its left side, carries warmer water toward colder areas; on its right side it carries colder water toward warmer areas. The counterclockwise whirl, on its right side, carries warmer water toward colder areas; on its left side it carries colder water toward warmer areas. The wave acts like the adjoining parts of the whirls.

point on earth moves toward the east at a rate of about 780 knots with the rotation of the earth. Now the parcel moves to latitude 40° N, about the latitude of Indianapolis.

Indianapolis is nearer the axis of rotation of the earth. Physics tells us that to maintain the same angular momentum it had in New Orleans the parcel of air would now have to speed up, to 880 knots eastward. But here the ground moves with its speed of rotation, slower than in New Orleans, at the rate of 690 knots.

The direct northward transfer of heat would appear to an observer on the ground in Indianapolis as an eastward movement of air at 880 minus 690—that is, 190—knots, what we would call a west wind of 190 knots. That most unlikely wind speed is another argument against straight line transfer of energy poleward.

The similarity of the circulation in a dishpan and improbably high wind speeds are not proof.

So other researchers used an entirely different approach. They programmed a computer with the basic laws of the atmosphere. To start with, the atmosphere was assumed at rest everywhere, and everywhere at the same temperature. Then they added sunshine to warm the air at the intensity and length of day appropriate for each latitude. The computer was instructed to draw a weather map of the conditions at the end of one day of sunshine. From that map, and one more day of added sunshine, the computer drew the second day's weather map. And so on. Computers are very good at such tasks. After a run of only thirty days of sunshine, the computer produced a weather map that looked as if it had been drawn from one day's actual observations.

The computer drew the easterly trade winds. Farther poleward it indicated prevailing westerly winds with embedded clockwise and counterclockwise whirls—the anticyclones and cyclones, Highs and Lows of mid latitudes. Near both poles it also traced—correctly—easterly winds again.

Both the dishpan experiment and the computer simulation are gross oversimplifications. We have a single medium, water or air, carry all the energy poleward. On the real earth the wind carries the main burden, but currents in the oceans help. In and near the tropics ocean currents carry fully one third of the heat load. Those are the North and the South Equatorial Currents and their feeder and offshoot currents in the Indian, Pacific, and Atlantic oceans. Even at latitude 50° N, ocean currents—e.g., the successor of the Gulf Stream in the English Channel—still carry an estimated 15 per cent of the total heat transferred. But that's a minor point, especially since the surface currents are mostly driven by the wind.

More important: Neither the dishpan nor the original computer model had mountains, land and water areas, snow or ice fields.

It is to be expected that mountains such as the Rockies, reaching halfway through the part of the atmosphere where the common winds blow, and lying right across the path of the prevailing westerly winds, must have an important influence on winds on both sides of them.

It is also to be expected that the sun will have a different effect when it shines on a region covered with forests rather than sand. The forest soaks up radiation greedily, while sand reflects a lot of it.

By far the greatest difference comes from the surface being water rather than land. Even when the sand on a Florida beach gets too hot to walk on barefoot, it is still night-cool a couple of inches (say 5 cm) below the surface. A couple of hours after sunset the surface of the same sand will be the temperature of the air.

The oceans act quite differently. Walk a few steps into the water and your feet and chest will normally signal the same temperature. It isn't that water conducts the heat from the surface so much better than sand. It's that the waves constantly mix the water heated at the surface with cooler water below. Go for a midnight swim, and the water will feel even warmer than in daytime. That's an illusion brought on by the cooler air. A thermometer will normally show exactly the same temperature as it did at sunset. Take the thermometer into the water a few days, or even weeks, later; it will show little change—there is such a depth and expanse of water to be cooled or heated. That explains why in spring the ocean seems to take forever to get warmer, why in the fall it stays comfortable long after lolling on the beach has become unattractive.

Freshly fallen snow reflects some 80 per cent of the sun's radiation; old snow perhaps 60 per cent. So only 20–40 per cent of our averaged incoming energy is available to melt either.

There is another factor. It takes energy to convert water from its solid state—snow or ice—to the liquid phase. A lot of energy, as anyone has found out when he tried to get water from snow in a ski hut or, worse, over an open fire. If you measured it, not in an inefficient cauldron but out of the wind in a laboratory, you'd find it takes about as much energy as it takes to bring the same quantity of water from room temperature to boiling. That's why winter seems to hang on forever in some places.

Mountains, soil, vegetation, oceans, snow and ice must greatly influence the weather. Not just locally but on a global scale. The surprise is that the featureless dishpan or computer model can give us an almost true picture of the general circulation.

10

Highs, Lows, and Winds

From the time of the invention of the barometer, people noticed that during bad weather the glass is usually low, that in settled weather the glass is usually high. That's why you still find the words RAIN, CHANGE, FAIR on barometers sold to the general public.

The words and their placement on the barometer are not scientific. Don't blame the earlier barometer makers, from whom the layout is copied. Science did not find the full explanation of the link between the level of the barometer and the weather until this century.

But if you predicted worse weather in the next couple of days when you saw the mercury drop, or forecast better weather to come soon on seeing it rise, you would have been right much more often than wrong.

Astute observers also noticed that often before high winds the glass rose or fell rapidly. The more rapidly, the stronger the winds were likely to blow.

People must also have realized early that weather and storms traveled. Sea captains met in grog shops and talked about storms they had run into on a recent voyage. Scientists kept diaries and corresponded with scientists in other lands. It must also have occurred to someone that the hurricane that devastated Puerto Rico on St. Anne's Day (July 26) might have been the same storm that had struck Antigua on St. James's Day (July 25) in the same year. (Hurricanes then were named after the saint on whose day they struck.)

The first written mention of the travel of storm is credited to Daniel Defoe, author of *Robinson Crusoe*. He connected the devastating storm of November 1703 in Great Britain with a storm that had lashed the seaboard of the American colonies a few days earlier.

The crucial discovery came from Benjamin Franklin. On October 21, 1743, he was looking forward to observing an eclipse of the moon in his telescope. In the afternoon a northeaster hit Philadelphia. Clouds would obscure the moon that night. He was surprised to learn later that in Boston—300 miles (480 km) northeast of Philadelphia—the storm didn't move in until everybody had seen the eclipse. The wind blew from the northeast, but the weather moved from the southwest!

In 1747 Franklin was to write, "Storms travel from Virginia to Connecticut, and then to Cape Sable on their northeasterly track." In a book published two hundred years later you might read, "In general, weather systems over the eastern United States travel from south of west to the north of east."

If weather systems didn't travel with the observed wind, the St. Anne's hurricane over Puerto Rico—which started with gales out of the north—could well have moved in from Antigua, roughly from the east.

But it would be another century after Franklin before the true relationship between the winds and traveling weather systems was solved. In the meantime data had to be collected.

The most systematic collection of weather data over the oceans is due to Lieutenant Matthew F. Maury. In 1842, sidelined from active sea duty by a leg injury, he was put in charge of the United States Navy's Depot of Charts and Instruments. This impressive-sounding office had been established twelve years earlier and assigned a complete staff: one lieutenant and one midshipman.

Maury started by dividing the charts of the oceans into areas 5 degrees of latitude by 5 degrees of longitude. Near the equator that gives squares 300 nautical miles (about 550 km) on a side. Farther away from the equator these areas change to rectangles on the chart, the longer side—in the north-south direction—300 miles long. For every ocean he ruled twelve charts—one for each month—in this manner.

In the proper rectangle he'd enter the direction and force of the wind experienced by a ship in that area in that month, and the barometric pressure recorded on that ship on that day. His first data came from ships' logs stored at the depot, some going back to 1784. Later he handed out forms to be filled in by shipmasters.

He then calculated for each rectangle the percentage of time winds were reported from each direction, and their average force. When he plotted the averaged monthly barometric pressure in the rectangles, he soon realized that the general circulation of the winds, both in direction and in strength, is governed by areas of high and low pressures. His *Wind and Current Chart of the North Atlantic*, published in 1847, was the first of the Navy's worldwide Pilot Charts, which to this day give credit to Maury's work.

While Maury plotted the winds over the oceans, James P. Espy, another American, charted storms over land, using records of the 1780–1840 period. For one 1840 storm he plotted not only direction and speed of the wind but also the temperature and barometric pressure at every observing station. His charts firmly proved two facts: Storms generally travel from west to east. And the storm was likely to be the strongest at the station where the barometer had dropped the most.

A third wind fact was added in 1857 by C. H. D. Buys Ballot (a double-barreled Dutch name, best pronounced "bice ba-*lott*"). He derived the "law" named after him by observation, unaware that William Ferrel, an American, had found it on theoretical grounds several months earlier.

Buys Ballot's law, also known as the law of storms, in its simplest form states: When you stand with your back to the wind, you'll have higher pressure on your right, lower pressure on your left. That applies to the northern hemisphere; south of the equator you'd have to face the wind, or switch the words left and right.

On an ocean, or a large lake, the *highest* pressure will be 15–25 degrees behind your right shoulder (in the northern hemisphere). The *lowest* pressure will be the same amount ahead of your left shoulder. This last rule, with its counterpart for the southern hemisphere, has saved uncounted lives at sea. It enabled a ship's master to locate—and sail away from—a hurricane, a relatively small area of extremely low pressure, as you'll see later.

Over land, near the surface, the angle the wind makes with your shoulders is greater yet, 30–40 degrees.

For the northern hemisphere, where most of my readers are likely to live, I have made up a memory aid for a person standing back to the wind (the sensible stance, especially in a hurricane): *High, right, rear; and low, left, leading.*

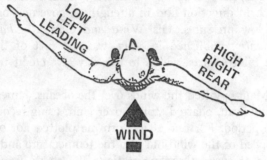

15. Buys Ballot's law

These rules, without doubt, were the most powerful tools for explaining and forecasting winds in the temperate zones.

Telegraph lines had begun to link cities. (The first one, between Washington and Baltimore, had gone into operation in 1844.) It was now possible to get distant weather observations quickly. And one could plot conditions at each observing station as soon as the messages started to come in over the telegraph.

To get a clear view of the pressure distribution over the country, the weatherman would draw lines connecting all stations that reported the same barometer reading (after correction for the height of the observer above sea level). These lines—the isobars—had to make the proper angle to the direction of the wind everywhere. That gave a convenient check for wrong readings, or errors in transmission. Better yet: It showed how to draw the isobars in areas between observations. You simply traced them downwind, at the proper angle to the wind direction at the nearest observing stations.

Even better: If you estimated the movement of the pressure system in the next twenty-four hours, you could predict tomorrow's wind direction at any point of your weather map. You estimated that movement from the general rule (toward the northeast), from its movement in the last twenty-four hours, from past experience in that area and season, or a combination of these techniques.

The *speed* of the wind followed another simple rule: The closer the spacing of the isobars, the stronger the wind. That again gave you a check on readings and transmission errors in the telegraphed observations. And it let you forecast strong winds whenever closely spaced isobars were likely to pass into the area for which you made the forecast. The movement of closely spaced isobars would make the barometer there fall (or rise) rapidly. That explains the already known relation between rapid change of atmospheric pressure and strong winds.

Most television weather people don't show isobars on their maps, just Highs and Lows. It's a lot of work to draw in those lines, and they clutter up the screen. But some newspaper maps show the isobars and some wind arrows. On such maps you can check the rules for direction and speed of the wind for yourself.

Today the Weather Service gets upper-air observations from balloons released at many civilian and military airports, naval stations, and ships. The meteorologist—or his computer—then draws lines similar to isobars on the weather map.

The difference between the lines drawn and isobars is a technicality. Instead of a plot of the barometric pressure at, say, 18,000 feet (or 5,500 m) at each station, the map will show at what height the balloon was when it reported a pressure of exactly 500 millibars. One reason for that procedure lies in the method of measurement.

The balloon carries a switch that closes at certain standard pressures (850, 700, 500, 400, . . . mb). Whenever the contact closes, the instrument package carried by the balloon reports humidity and temperature at that level by radio. The balloon is followed from the ground. That gives the height of the balloon (and permits the calculation of the wind direction and speed).

When all the stations that reported the 500-mb pressure at, say,

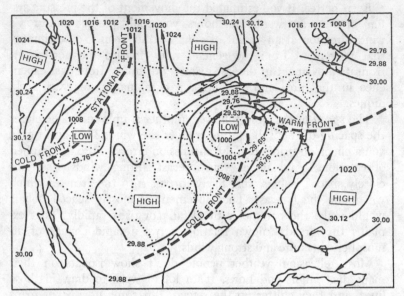

16. Newspaper weather map. Solid lines connect points of the same barometric pressure. These isobars here are labeled in both inches of mercury and millibars. Arrows indicate general wind flow.

17,900 feet are connected on the map, we get the 17,900 *contour*. That name for the isoheight line is apt. When other contours—e.g., for 18,100, 18,300, . . .—are drawn, we get a map that shows the 500-mb surface as a topographic map shows the elevation of the land by contours (figure 17).

On the contour maps of all upper levels the wind will obey the strict Buys Ballot law. It keeps high pressure exactly to the right, low pressure exactly to the left. Without any angle. (Except for some minor effects you'll read about presently.)

Put differently: The wind flows *parallel* to the contour lines.

That sentence was easy to write and is easy to read. But its meaning is startling: The wind doesn't flow from higher pressure toward lower pressure, but straight in between them. It is the equivalent of saying, "Water doesn't flow downhill; it flows *around* hills maintaining the same level."

I could start by saying that on these charts the hills aren't very

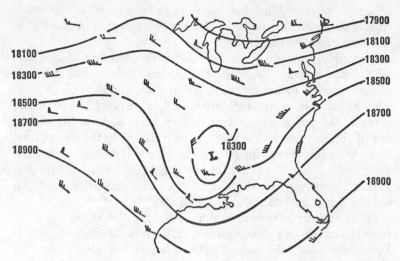

17. Upper-air map. Contour lines connect points where 500-millibar pressure is found at same height (labeled in feet) above sea level.

Arrows flying with the wind indicate wind direction. Wind speed is shown by flags and feathers. Each flag means 50 knots; each full feather 10 knots; each half-feather 5 knots.

high, the valleys not very deep. On a 500-mb map you may find a hill 1,200 feet (370 m) above the average level, a valley that much below it. And they are 1,500 miles (2,400 km) apart. That makes for a very gentle slope, about 3:10,000—or about 1.6 feet per mile (30 cm per km). You wouldn't expect water to *rush* down such a slope. But it would flow. Why doesn't air?

I could point out the limp in the analogy of water running from hills to valleys. These features of the landscape are there all the time. But high and low pressures form gradually. If the air rushed from high to low pressure, high pressure wouldn't have a chance to build. Any beginning low pressure would soon be equalized and disappear from the weather map.

But you are entitled to the full explanation. For that I have to bring in something called the Coriolis effect, or Coriolis force (after the French mathematician who described it in 1836). Let me state the principle as simply as possible: Due to the rotation of the earth, everything that moves in the northern hemisphere is turned somewhat to the right of its straight path. (In the southern hemisphere, to the left.)

I strongly urge you to accept that without trying to find out why. Some authors, to make that strange effect clear to their readers, shoot a rocket from the North Pole, aimed at New York. The rocket will miss that city and land near Chicago. True enough. But you might explain that by New York having moved out of the way due to the rotation of earth while the rocket traveled. A similar rocket fired from the South Pole toward Buenos Aires, will come down left of its target—in Chile or into the Pacific. Again you might think of the duck missed because you did not "lead" it when you aimed your gun.

Other authors invite you to draw a straight line toward or away from the center of a slowly turning disk, say a phonograph record. You know what will happen. The rotation will spoil your aim. You'll draw a curve.

But neither rocket nor phonograph explains what happens when you fire a rocket from Philadelphia due west toward California. It will turn to the right of its intended trajectory and land in British Columbia.

The Coriolis effect depends on your latitude. It is strongest near the poles, becomes negligible near the equator. It also depends on the speed and the length of time taken in travel.

An example: Halfway between the North Pole and the equator—the latitude of Minneapolis—driving your automobile at 55 mph (90 km/h) you should be 18 feet to the right after one mile's travel (3.5 meters after one kilometer). Your tires resist that sideways motion. And, anyway, you'd compensate for it by steering slightly to the left. Just as an aircraft pilot does, unknowingly.

Here's a more surprising example: You are walking in the same latitude at 4 mph (6.5 km/h). After one mile you'll be 250 feet off to the right (48 meters after one kilometer). Your speed in that example was low, but you gave this pseudo force a quarter of an hour to work on you.

In either example it makes no difference in which direction you proceed, south or west or any other. You'll always be set to the right.

Air in motion, which we call wind, must show the same deflection as an automobile, a hiker, or a rocket. Under that influence the moving air will be turned from the expected "downhill" course from higher toward lower pressure.

It can be shown mathematically that between straight contour lines the turning and the downhill force will balance when—and only when—the air moves parallel to the contour lines.

That again is best taken on faith. If you had to write a textbook, you might explain it this way. A parcel of air on a high contour starts falling toward a lower contour. Like a falling stone it will accelerate. That simile is unimpeachable: Both the air parcel and the stone are in free fall under the influence of the force of gravity.

As the air parcel speeds up under the influence of gravity, the Coriolis effect will push it more and more to the right. That'll go on until the parcel of air moves at right angles to the fall line, the line you would have expected it to follow in free fall, the straight line from high to low pressure. It will then continue in a straight line, without speeding up or slowing down.

Or you could draw a picture showing the air parcel at point 1 at the start and then follow it through points 2, 3, ... That would look very scientific. The wind, of course, has no such diagram. It probably never "starts" to blow; it has been blowing all along. If now its speed changes, it adjusts to the Coriolis effect as automatically as the moving pinball adjusts to gravity when you tilt the machine. The effect: The wind flows parallel to the contour lines (with high pressure on its right in the northern hemisphere).

That's what makes it so easy to draw wind arrows on an upper air map after the contour lines have been drawn for that barometric level. The weatherman, or his computer, can also draw the contour lines from the known wind direction aloft. He just draws them parallel to the wind.

Wind speed aloft follows the rule of winds near the surface: The closer the spacing of the isolines—isobars or contours—the stronger the wind.

The actual wind speed aloft is always within a few per cent of the speed one can calculate from the spacing of the contours and the latitude. The direction of the actual wind aloft is always within a few degrees of being parallel to the contour lines.

The wind calculated from pressure difference and adjusted for the rotation of the earth—the Coriolis effect—is called *geostrophic* (earth-turned) wind. Why is the actual wind aloft not *exactly* geostrophic in speed and direction? It's not the fault of the laws applied, but due to two other causes. Temperatures aloft are not uniform over the entire map. That by itself, without any pressure differences, would cause *thermal* winds. When you combine the thermal wind with the geostrophic wind, you'll get a wind that differs a bit from the pure geostrophic.

Also the contour lines are not straight as we had assumed earlier. Where they curve sharply, you have to take into consideration the centrifugal effect, the push you feel when you take a curve at high speed.

Aloft the wind blows virtually parallel to the lines that indicate atmospheric pressure differences. Why does it make an angle with the isobars on the surface map? Why to apply Buys Ballot's law on the ground do you have to swivel your shoulders? The answer: friction.

Aloft the wind balanced pressure force and Coriolis effect. Now near the ground, friction slows it. As it slows, the Coriolis effect—which, as we have seen, depends on speed—weakens. It no longer balances pressure. The wind changes direction, takes up the more expected course from higher to lower pressure. It crosses the isobars.

You may wonder how high up the winds are parallel to the pressure lines, at what level they begin to feel friction, slow down, and turn toward lower pressure. The answer: at about 3,000 feet (1,000 m). That's surprising. One might think friction would begin at the level of tree tops or roofs. But here we are dealing with gases. Ocean waves, rough ground, bushes . . . create little eddies in the air, which create more eddies higher up, leading to more eddies . . . right up to the level given.

So the friction spreads upward from the surface as it were, but of course with diminishing effect. That leads to a gradual slowing and turning of the wind between that level and the ground. You can often observe the gradual shift of the wind by just watching a kite rising higher and higher.

The friction—or eddy making—over water is less than over land. Over the ocean the surface wind will be slowed to about two thirds of the geostrophic speed; over land to about half of the upper air speed.

This lesser slowing from geostrophic speed over water also explains why winds over water deviate less from the geostrophic wind direction than over land—why you don't have to swivel your shoulders as much to apply the law of storms over water.

All of this is summarized in the accompanying table.

Aloft	Near surface	
(above 3,000 ft [1,000 m])	Over water	Over land
WIND DIRECTION: Higher pressure to right in northern hemisphere; to left in southern hemisphere.		
Virtually parallel to pressure contours.	Crosses isobars toward lower pressure at 15°–20° angle.	Crosses isobars toward lower pressure at 30°–40° angle.
WIND SPEED: Virtually geostrophic.	⅔ geostrophic.	½ geostrophic.

Let's use this information and pretend we are looking over the shoulders of a forecaster.

On the surface forecast map in latitude of New York (about 40° N) the isobars drawn at 4-mb (0.12 inch of mercury) intervals are 350 nautical miles apart. From that the weatherman could calculate the geostrophic wind speed: 10 knots. Actually he uses a transparent scale, lays it on the map between two isobars, and directly reads the geostrophic wind speed for that latitude.

Two thirds of that gives a wind speed of 6.7 knots over water. Since the winds don't blow steadily at the same rate, he'll forecast

5–10 knots for the marine area. Since the ratio of two thirds to one half is about the same as statute miles to nautical miles, he'll forecast 5–10 mph (8–16 km/h) winds for the land area. (The exact calculation of one half the geostrophic wind speed converted to statute miles per hour would have given 5.8 mph [9 km/h] and led to the same forecast.)

On the forecast map the isobars tend SW to NE, with the higher pressure on the northern side. The geostrophic wind will be northeast, parallel to the isolines with higher pressure on the right. The surface wind will be at an angle to the geostrophic wind, crossing the isobars away from higher and toward lower pressure. The angle will be about 15–25 degrees over water, 30–40 degrees over land. Since the wind doesn't blow steadily from the

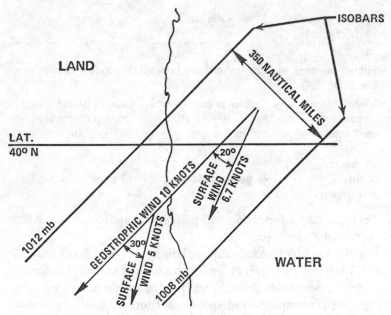

18. Predicting the wind from isobars

same direction, you'd be justified in forecasting north to northeast winds for both land and marine areas.

The isobars usually are not neat straight lines. When they curve gently you can still forecast wind direction from their general trend.

But sometimes the Lows and Highs are circular (or elliptical), as small as a hurricane or as large as the Bermuda High, which at times covers most of the North Atlantic. For such situations it is often useful to remember two rules:

Around Highs, winds flow clockwise and slightly outward.

Around Lows, winds flow counterclockwise and slightly inward.

Using these rules and looking at a newspaper weather map that shows isobars, you can fill in the winds in any area that interests you. From the predicted motion of the Highs and Lows—often shown by arrows on such maps—you can predict how the winds will be blowing when the pressure centers have moved.

You can even estimate the wind direction from maps on your television screen even if they only show Highs and Lows. For a

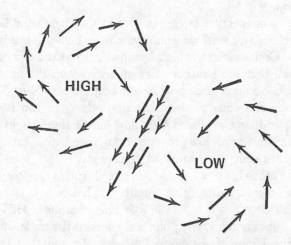

19. Winds around circular High and Low. Around the High, circulation is clockwise; around the Low, counterclockwise. Note that the wind between them is a continuation of *both* these motions.

first approximation, assume they are circular with the center where the letters H and L appear, and apply the above rules.

If the weatherperson shows you where these centers are expected to be tomorrow, you can repeat the process around the new positions and get a rough forecast.

Without any map, stand with your back to the wind and apply the right-rear-high and left-leading-low method to locate the pressure centers approximately. Then proceed as if you had the letters H and L marked on a map. If you lack any better information, assume the centers will move toward the northeast.

A question may have occurred to you: Can we explain the trade winds say in the southern North Atlantic as flow around the southern flank of the Bermuda (or Azores, or North Atlantic) High? That seems tempting. Especially if you happen to know that a similar high-pressure area covers the Pacific, summer and winter. You become convinced that your theory must be right when you find corresponding high-pressure areas in the southern hemisphere, spanning the Atlantic, Pacific, and Indian oceans the year round.

There's a connection of course. But in the trade wind belts the simple rules don't work as accurately as in higher latitudes. Reason: The Coriolis effect, which becomes zero at the equator, here is so small that the weatherman's standard tool, the geostrophic wind scale, becomes useless at about latitude 20° N or S. There and nearer the equator the surface winds cross the isobars at changing and large angles as they flow out of these Highs and toward the equatorial low-pressure trough and the Intertropical Convergence Zone, the area of the doldrums.

On the other hand, what you have read in this chapter does explain the *polar easterlies*, briefly mentioned before.

Cold air descends near the North Pole creating a High, much as the air descending at the poleward edges of the trade wind belts creates the Highs of the horse latitudes. Around that High the circulation is clockwise. Clockwise circulation around the North Pole means easterly winds.

Over the South Pole, where the circulation is counterclockwise around the corresponding High, that again gives easterly winds. You can verify that on a globe.

The polar easterlies are not as constant as the trade winds. Like the prevailing westerlies of the temperate zones, they are often interrupted by winds from all other directions.

11

Air Masses and Fronts

Long before scientists made models of the atmosphere in rotating dishpans or on electronic computers, people noticed how different winds felt on different days. On a winter day in the American Midwest the wind seems to have come straight from the North Pole; on a summer day it may feel as if it had escaped from a sauna.

Theophrastus knew about the different feel of winds, as you have seen, and explained it plausibly. But only in this century has weather science come up with the complete explanation: air masses.

When air stays over a large land area of uniform temperature, it takes on the characteristics of the conditions there. When it stays, or travels, over an expanse of ocean—always at virtually the same temperature—it takes on the personality of that area.

You'll expect air that has been conditioned over land to be dry, air modified by a stay or passage over water to be moist. You are right, of course. Air from a cold continent typically contains 2 parts of water vapor in 1,000 parts of air; the common variety of maritime air typically carries 18 parts of water vapor.

And you know that air from the arctic regions will be cold, from the tropics warm.

So far no spectacular discoveries. But here is the important concept: A body of air tends to keep its personality after it has moved away from the area where its character has been shaped. On the ground the body of air will betray its origin by its temperature and its moisture content. They will be virtually the same over hundreds of miles (or kilometers) in all directions. (Sometimes a single air mass will cover the United States from coast to coast, or from the Canadian border to the Gulf of Mexico.)

Above the ground, as you go higher, the temperature will drop in any air mass. But the *rate* of this temperature drop is also a characteristic of that type of air mass. If that rate changes at a given level, as in an inversion, that too is a signature of the air mass. To the weatherman, that's as clear as if a tag had been tied to it saying, "I was formed over a tropical sea."

On weather maps you may find air masses identified by a combination of letters: c for continental, m for maritime, P for polar, and T for tropical. That makes four combinations possible: cP for continental polar, mP for maritime polar, cT for continental tropical, and mT for maritime tropical air masses. Occasionally you'll find another letter added: w for air warmer than the ground over which it now lies, k for colder. These letters are added after the two letters that describe the most common air masses—e.g., mTw.

Occasionally you'll find a single letter identifying an air mass: A for arctic—or antarctic in the southern hemisphere—(continental), E for equatorial (maritime), and S for superior (a warm dry air mass having originated aloft).

Continental polar air (cP) may have been conditioned over Alaska, Canada, or Siberia. From that you can see that "polar" here really means subpolar, or what you might call arctic. But arctic (A) here refers to an air mass even colder and drier than continental polar, formed in the belt of the easterly winds around the pole.

In winter continental polar air, having crossed the northern border, is familiar almost everywhere in the United States. Several times each winter it spreads its cold to southern Florida and across the Gulf of Mexico in a "norther."

Maritime polar air (mP) in winter is relatively mild, in summer it is decidedly cool. It enters the United States through the Pacific Northwest, sometimes through California, and occasionally through New England.

Continental tropical air (cT), hot and dry, is conditioned over subtropical land masses: the southwestern United States, Mexico, and (in summer) central Asia.

Maritime tropical air (mT), warm and moist, from the Atlantic covers the eastern and central United States a good part of every summer. The even warmer and moister maritime tropical air entering from the Gulf of Mexico causes sticky days, thunderstorms, and tornadoes in the Mississippi basin and beyond.

Air masses, after having moved into the United States, often stay over one place for several days. They are often so large that even when they move you'll have the same weather for several days: pleasant days, or a cold wave, or a heat wave.

By staying over one area an air mass gradually changes character. A frigid continental polar air mass in winter passing over the United States gets warmed by contact with the less cold land. By the time the air from Canada reaches southern Florida in a typical norther it has warmed from well below freezing to perhaps 50° F (10° C).

So air masses do change. A dry cold air mass from Siberia (cP) crossing the Pacific warms and absorbs moisture. It reaches British Columbia or the Washington coast as mP air. Still traveling westward, it runs into mountains. It is lifted, discharges moisture, and gets warmed by the foehn or chinook effect described in Chapter 7; on the leeward side of the mountains it continues as warm dry air.

A maritime tropical air mass coming in from the Gulf of Mexico in summer shows much less change. There are no mountains to wring the moisture from it. The land is cooler than the air. But the cooled bottom layer just lies there. Cool air doesn't rise; there is little mixing. That's why a spell of hot muggy days in the south central and midwestern states is likely to last, and last.

But the weather eventually does change. What brings the change? On a more sophisticated level: Air masses, in general, are areas of high barometric pressure; such Highs, as you read in the last chapter, have a clockwise wind circulation, and normally clear skies. Then where do the Lows, with counterclockwise circulation, and generally bad weather come from?

The answer was supplied—in rigorous mathematical form—by Jakob Bjerknes in Norway toward the end of World War I. The period probably suggested the key word in the explanation: fronts.

Contrary to what one might expect, air masses that form side by side, or come together by their individual motions, do not mix. Their common border is called a front. Surface weather maps, in the newspaper or on television, show these fronts prominently.

Where a colder air mass takes over territory on the surface formerly occupied by warmer air, the weather map shows a *cold front* (a line spiked with triangles pointing in the direction of the movement of the front).

Where a warmer air mass invades territory on the surface formerly held by colder air, the weather map shows a *warm front* (a line on which roost half circles pointing in the direction of the movement of the front).

Where an air mass shows little tendency at the moment to invade the territory of its neighbor, the weather map shows a stationary front (a line with triangles on one side, half circles on the other; that's logical enough).

Whenever a front—cold or warm—passes you, you'll experience a sudden shift in wind direction. In the northern hemisphere that shift in either frontal passage will be clockwise, with the sun. Typically from northeast to southeast, or from southwest to northwest.

From the last chapter you'll remember the relation between surface wind and isobars. The sudden shift at a front means that the isobars, which normally are smooth curves, must show a kink at the front.

The weatherman who places the front on today's weather map has had many other indications of the approaching front: yesterday's map; high clouds ahead of the front where warm air was lifted to the condensation level ahead of a bulldozing cold front, or even farther ahead where warm air aloft climbs over cold air long before the warm front makes itself felt on the surface; lower clouds and perhaps precipitation as the front approached; sharply different temperatures reported from stations ahead and behind the front; and different moisture content of the air masses, indicated by the dew point reports from the same stations.

You'll see one or more patterns similar to the one shown in figure 20 on almost every weather map. You can tell the direction of the wind around the system from the isobars and the rules

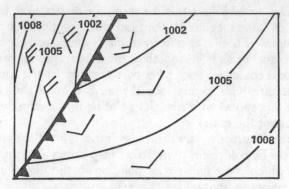

20. Winds at a front. Note how the isobars break
at the front. Therefore the wind direction—indicated by the arrows—suddenly changes at the front.
Ahead of the front it is from the southwest, behind
the front from the northwest. A cold front is shown
here, but the shift is similar at a warm front.

given in the preceding chapter. The speed of the wind will be
lowest where the isobars are far apart, highest where they are
closest together.

During their lifetime—several days—these disturbances undergo
typical changes, first described in detail by Bjerknes. Let's follow
one such system, as illustrated in figure 21.

It starts with two air masses peacefully side by side, separated
by a stationary front.

That peaceful state is not likely to last long. The air flow in one
air mass "rubbing" against the flow in the other will cause a wave.
Just as wind passing over water causes waves.

If conditions are right, the wave once started will grow. The
angle (in the originally straight boundary line) closes to form a
warm front, and behind it a cold front.

The wind flow around the point where the two fronts meet becomes stronger; the isobars are now spaced closer together. The direction of the wind is counterclockwise around that point. That's
typical of a low-pressure area.

But then some change can be expected. Cold fronts travel faster
than warm fronts. The cold front on the surface map will seem to

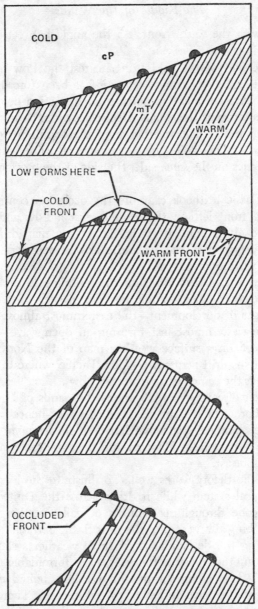

21. Development of a wave cyclone. Note the symbols for cold and warm fronts (e.g., in second view), stationary front (top), and occluded front (top of last view).

catch up with the warm front. As the angle between the fronts closes, the Low intensifies.

Soon the part of the cold front nearest the Low reaches the warm front. All the warm surface air has been forced aloft; the two fronts have become one north of the junction point. On the satellite photographs the clouds themselves often clearly trace that pattern. On the surface weather map the common front, called an *occluded* (pinched-off) front, is shown as a line with triangles and half circles on the *same* side, the side of the movement of the system.

In the classic textbook example the occlusion continues until there is no front left on the ground, just a Low and its counterclockwise circulation of winds. That Low may drift on, and eventually merge with the Icelandic Low, a semipermanent feature of the weather map.

But often a new wave forms on the trailing cold front, and the whole cycle starts anew. Whole families of such related Lows in various stages of development—the easternmost almost totally occluded, the westernmost just forming an open wave—can sometimes be seen on a surface weather map of the North Atlantic. Similar systems drift across the North Pacific, where the Aleutian Low serves as the cemetery for overaged Lows.

Since their discovery in 1918, many thousands of Lows formed along the border of two air masses as a wave—hence called wave cyclones (cyclone being a somewhat obsolete synonym of Low in this phrase)—have been followed and their life cycle more or less accurately forecast.

Overall, the theory works well. To illustrate the life cycle of a simple, typical system while it drifts across the United States, I have just gone through six months of daily weather maps. No luck. Something always spoiled the neat classic pattern.

Forecasting the development of these weather systems, which follow one another most of the year, faces formidable difficulties. The first: Where along a thousand-mile-long boundary between air masses will a wave form? A partial answer: There are land areas over which that process is more likely than elsewhere. Examples: in the lee of the Rocky Mountains, from Colorado to Alberta; over the Ozarks; and along the east coast of the United States, especially near Cape Hatteras.

The next question: In what direction will the disturbance travel? The general storm tendency is a first approximation. You'd probably make a better forecast by continuing yesterday's travel. An even better forecast is possible. Every weather station reports the amount of rise or fall of its barometric pressure since its last observation. Most often the Low will travel in the direction from the station reporting the greatest rise toward the station reporting the greatest fall.

Will the Low deepen, that is intensify? Or perhaps fill, that is weaken? That also affects the system's forward speed. (Deepening Lows slow.) Does it approach an area of high pressure that will block its progress?

It is a monument to the genius of Bjerknes that he worked out the model of the wave cyclone knowing almost nothing about what is going on higher up in the atmosphere.

What is going on there? You'll get a first glimpse of that in the next chapter.

12

Jet Streams

At dawn on November 24, 1944, a dozen squadrons of B-29s—more than one hundred planes—carrying three hundred tons of bombs took off from Saipan in the Marianas. Their target: an aircraft-engine plant in Tokyo, 1,500 nautical miles to the north. They were to bomb from 30,000 feet (about 9,000 m), approaching their target from the west.

As they neared Japan, they ran into increasingly stronger westerly winds. On their bombing run they were swept along by a 120-knot tail wind. To make things worse, visibility was bad. Low clouds obscured the landmarks they had been briefed about. One third of the planes never saw the sprawling target and had to rely on radar. Only about one plane in five released its bombs near the engine plant. The unexpectedly strong wind spoiled the aim. Damage to the plant was negligible.

A mission three days later had a similar experience. Winds measured at more than 200 knots joined the antiaircraft guns and fighter planes in the defense of Tokyo.

We now know that these unexpected winds were neutral. Their first known victim was a German photo-reconnaissance plane cruising above the range of guns and fighter planes over the Mediterranean. It had exhausted its fuel supply in bucking strong head winds. Out of fuel, it had to ditch. That plane at least had had some warning: The weather observer on the ground had reported 170-knot west winds before he lost sight of his weather balloon.

Before planes flew at these high levels, these winds were not suspected. Few balloon observations had given a hint of such high-velocity winds. Clouds often got between the weather balloon and the theodolite with which the ground observer tried to track it. The highest wind speeds occur in rather narrow bands and so were also missed by the occasional manned balloon flights.

These high-altitude, high-speed winds were later given the name the *jet stream*. A catchy name but triply misleading. There is, of course, no nozzle in the sky to produce a jet. It is not continuous, nor does it follow a set course as a river does. And there is not just one jet stream, but several.

These jet streams—there are generally three in winter and two in summer in each hemisphere—are a series of high-speed air flows, appearing here, disappearing there, and shifting position from day to day. Jets are thousands of miles (kilometers) long, hundreds of miles (kilometers) wide, and several thousand feet (a few thousand meters) deep.

After World War II, even before much of that was known, pilots of high-flying eastbound planes took advantage of these winds that could save them hours of flying time and tons of fuel. Once at a likely jet-stream altitude, the pilot would approach a possible jet at an angle until his instruments showed that he had found a strong tail wind. In his search the pilot was guided by sheets of feathery cirrus clouds that are often present on the warm side of a jet. In the northern hemisphere that would be the south side.

What exactly is a jet stream? Here is a simplified definition, based on the criteria of the World Meteorological Organization: a strong narrow air current in the upper troposphere (or above) that drops off rapidly in both horizontal and vertical direction. To qualify as a jet stream under WMO definition, the wind speed must be at least 30 meters per second, or about 58 knots.

The troposphere is the lower atmosphere, the stage where most of our weather performs, where temperature decreases with height. Its upper limit, where a constant temperature is reached, is called the *tropopause*. That's near 29,000 feet (9 km) over the subpolar regions—a little lower in winter, higher in summer. Over the tropics it is higher the year round. In mid latitudes you may expect to find the tropopause near 36,000 feet (11 km).

It's near these levels that you'll encounter the strongest wind, the "core" of each jet stream. Wind speeds will be of the order of

100 knots. Above and below that level the speed drops rapidly. It may diminish by 3 to 6 knots per thousand feet (5–10 m/sec per km). So a 100-knot stream in mid latitudes could lose its official jet status near 27,000 feet (8 km).

Across the stream the speed typically diminishes at a rate of 16 knots for every hundred statute miles from the core (5 m/s in 100 km). At that rate the 100-knot stream would drop below official jet speed about 250 miles from the core. Usually jet speed extends farther on the equatorial side than on the polar side of the core.

In length a jet stream may stay above the minimum speed limit for the width of a continent. It's compared to such lengths that a jet is a "narrow" air stream.

It's not difficult to visualize the dropping off of speed away from the center. The speed of surface current in every river drops from midstream to the banks. We can readily imagine the current in a river also dropping off toward the bottom. But in a jet stream the speed also diminishes upward.

The 100-knot jet used in the example might look like this: It could be as long as Canada is wide (about 3,000 miles), 4 miles deep, and 400 miles wide (say 250 miles on the right of the core, 150 miles on the left). An enormous, very flattened, somewhat lopsided snake.

What causes these strange winds? For a model let's go back to the dishpan described in Chapter 9.

We looked at a pan heated at the rim and cooled at the center. You watched the circulation of water in the pan when it stood still, rotated slowly, and rotated considerably faster. Now let's watch what happens between these two speeds of rotation.

When the pan first speeds up, a ring forms around the center. It does that even when the clumsy cooling cylinder is removed and replaced by some other means of chilling the center. (You could try pouring cement on the bottom of the pan and chilling that through the shaft.)

The explanation for the ring is this: Particles moving toward the center carry the momentum acquired near the rim. When they get near the center, their speed approaches the speed limit set by the internal friction in the water. That stops them from approaching closer to the center.

At what corresponds to latitude 80° on this flat model of the

earth, the ground speed of a particle would be six times the speed
at the rim, which simulates the equator; at latitude 85° the speed
in relation to the bottom of the pan would be twelve times the
speed at the periphery.

Now increase the speed of rotation of the pan. The limit set by
internal friction is reached sooner; the ring moves away from the
center. If you increase the speed some more, the ring develops
bumps and hollows and begins to resemble a cloverleaf. The entire pattern slowly revolves in the pan—from west to east if you
make the pan simulate the rotation of earth as seen from the
North Pole.

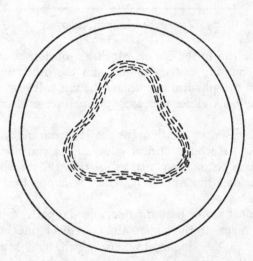

22. Clover pattern in the dishpan

If you gradually increase the speed, you'll get a four-leaf clover,
a five-leaf. . . . A seven-leaf clover has been raised in such a dishpan.

When you increase the speed somewhat more, the symmetry
breaks down. The leaves become lopsided, their central vein tend-
ing southwest to northeast. You can see hints of such a wave in
figure 13. Figure 23 shows one in detail.

You can see that this wave carries heat north, brings cold south.
Obviously the right arm of the wave also carries westerly momen-

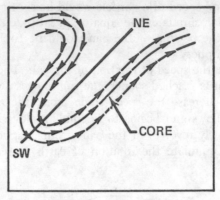

23. Wave in the dishpan, enlarged

tum from the rim to the center. Much less obviously, so does the
left arm by carrying *easterly* momentum the other way. Mathematically the two physical actions are the same. Just as depositing
money in the bank either increases your balance or decreases your
overdraft.

When the speed of rotation (or the temperature difference to
be evened out) reaches a critical value, such a wave becomes unstable. It leaves behind two "masses"—I called them whirls earlier
—rotating in opposite directions. Then it jumps to a new, less
looping path.

The multileaf clover patterns resemble the path of jet streams
on weather maps of the upper atmosphere of one hemisphere.
Right down to the sloping troughs, which tend southwest to
northeast in the northern hemisphere. And right down to the occasional large excursions toward the equator, the calving of two
masses—one rotating clockwise, one counterclockwise—followed
by a rapid adjustment to a more normal course of the jet stream.

We could have approached the explanation of jet streams from
another angle.

You know that over the middle half of the globe, on either side
of the equator in a zone three thousand nautical miles wide, temperatures are uniformly high, varying only a few degrees summer

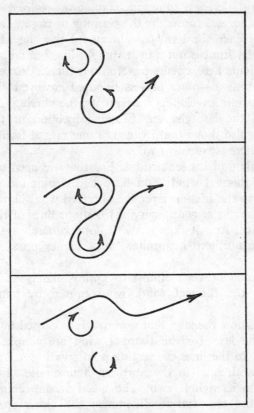

24. Wave becomes unstable, then leaves behind two whirls rotating in opposite directions and takes a less curving new path.

and winter. In a similar way, the polar caps in both hemispheres are zones of fairly uniform low temperatures.

Between the tropics and the polar cap of each hemisphere lies the zone of the disturbed westerly winds. These belts of disturbed westerlies roughly correspond to the temperate zones without their subtropical fringes.

It is in these two belts that all the temperature (and humidity) differences between polar and tropical air masses come together.

Even before Bjerknes, some meteorologists realized that our changing weather was caused by the clashing of tropical and polar air. Bjerknes coined the term *polar front* for the line where they meet. The polar front is not a neat straight line but on any given day shows salients here, enemy penetrations there. Worse, instead of being continuous—more or less oriented east-west—it breaks into many separate enveloping movements, the curving fronts you looked at in the last chapter. Closer inspection of the daily weather maps also shows that instead of one ragged front in each hemisphere, there are usually two.

None of this explains jet streams. For that we need one more concept: the thermal wind. You have had a hint already. You read that above the friction layer the observed wind blows *almost* parallel to (straight or gently curving) contour lines of the equal-pressure surface. And it does so with *approximately* geostrophic speed (in the northern hemisphere with higher pressure on its right).

The difference between almost or approximately and exactly is caused by the thermal wind, wind caused by temperature differences.

When you know the laws that govern winds caused by pressure differences, the laws for the thermal wind are simple. ONE: It blows parallel to the lines connecting points with equal temperatures, called isotherms (in the northern hemisphere with higher temperature on its right). TWO: The speed of the thermal wind depends on the temperature difference; the closer spaced the isotherms, the stronger the thermal wind.

It is no coincidence that the laws governing wind caused by temperature differences and by pressure differences are so similar. They are the same law: Whatever the driving force, the Coriolis effect, which turns everything that moves on the revolving earth— rockets, automobiles, and hikers—off its original path, turns the moving air, the wind. It stops turning the moving air only when it has succeeded in turning it at right angles to the force that drives it in the first place, higher pressure or higher temperature.

In his calculation the weatherman must combine the two winds, thermal and geostrophic. A simple problem in geometry. Air in motion, the wind, doesn't have to perform that operation.

It moves under the influence of *all* the forces that act on it. Just as on a windy day an apple doesn't have to combine gravity and wind drift to know where to land.

In a single air mass, almost by definition of uniform temperature at every level, thermal winds will be unimportant. But where air masses of different origin lie side by side, there will be a temperature difference at each constant pressure level. And the differences will get greater the higher you go. The thermal wind will increase in strength with height.

Here's an example: At latitude 45° a temperature difference of 3° F in a distance of 100 statute miles will cause an increase in wind speed of 20 knots for every 10,000 feet of altitude. (In metric units: A temperature difference of 1° C in a distance of 100 km will cause an increase of 10 m/s—or 20 knots—for every 3,000 m of altitude.) That alone—without any geostrophic wind—will give jet-stream velocity winds near the 30,000-foot (9,000-m) level.

You'll be most likely to find large temperature differences at the edge of the tropics and near the polar front. That explains two important jet streams in each hemisphere: the subtropical and the polar jet streams. The temperature contrast between air masses is likely to be greatest during that hemisphere's winter. And that's when the jet streams are strongest, up to 300 knots.

It was late November when the bomber pilots over Japan first encountered a jet stream. And there maritime tropical air lay next to polar air conditioned over Siberia.

There is yet another jet stream. One that develops over each pole during its winter, the polar-night jet. When after several months the sun rises again, it disappears; it then forms over the other pole, where the night is just beginning.

Don't think of any of these jet streams as fixed. They speed up and slow down. They throw large loops and straighten out. Sometimes a jet splits temporarily into two arms that reunite downwind like a river that flows around an island. At other times the subtropical jet stream and the polar jet stream in one hemisphere may merge into one.

Earlier you read that the jet streams are strongest near the tropopause, and that the tropopause is higher over the tropics than over the polar regions. But don't imagine the tropopause as a

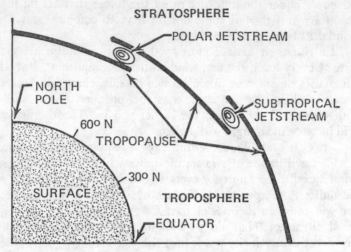

25. Jet streams and tropopause (scale in atmosphere greatly exaggerated)

blanket higher above your toes than over your stomach. It's more like the overlapping plates in a suit of armor. The chinks coincide with the area of the strongest jets. That fact is important to all life on earth, as you'll see in the last chapter.

Being high in the atmosphere, jet streams are not shown on the surface weather map. But the meanderings and other changes in the jet streams strongly influence wind and weather near the surface.

In the dishpan experiment you have seen how a tropical mass is carried poleward, far from its origin, and how a polar mass is carried toward the equator and then sloughed off. Jet streams in the atmosphere in the same manner bring together air masses of different origin and start a process that near the ground is indistinguishable from that of the formation of a wave cyclone and its development discussed in the preceding chapter. That similarity accounts for much of the success of the Bjerknes model in day-to-day forecasting before jet streams had even been discovered.

That's not just in some theoretical model. In winter the polar jet is almost always over the United States. In summer it retreats to Canada; then the subtropical jet also moves somewhat north and touches the southern states.

Meteorologists, starting with C. G. Rossby, have unlocked some other mysteries of the upper atmosphere. Waves in the pressure contours on upper-air maps, resembling the multiple clover leaves and tilted troughs produced in the dishpan, and the behavior of the jet streams are now routine tools of the weather forecaster. They let him predict the movement of air masses, formation of surface Lows, their progress across the map, and their deepening and filling.

That's how he, or his computer, predicts—among other things— the speed and direction of the wind for tomorrow.

13

Unusual Winds: Hurricanes

We know exactly when Western man first learned about hurricanes. Columbus brought that knowledge back from the West Indies. That's no surprise. Hurricanes don't occur in Europe. Australia, where such winds are now called cyclones or willy-willies, had not yet been discovered. The tropical cyclones of the Indian Ocean, the typhoons of the western Pacific (sometimes called baguios in the Philippines)—all these hurricanes under different names were far off.

We now know that these destructive storms occur over and near all tropical oceans except the South Atlantic. And that they are more common in the western stretches of these oceans.

Detailed knowledge about these storms was acquired slowly, hindered by the fact that so many ships that experienced them— or even only their fringe winds—never returned. By international agreement we now distinguish between *tropical storms*, with wind speeds of 17–32 m/s (33–62 knots), and *hurricanes* (or typhoons), with wind speeds greater than 32 m/s. The United States Weather Service uses slightly different figures and adds another category: *tropical depressions*, with wind speeds below those of a tropical storm.

As records of these destructive storms accumulated it became clear that there were areas and seasons where these winds were most frequent.

Seamen and land-based observers catalogued the signs that gave warning. One sign: a wind from an unusual direction, the normal easterly flow of the trade winds replaced by winds from the southwest, west, northwest, or north. Another sign: a high deck of feathery cirrus clouds, mare's-tails. Afloat, unusually high seas and swells—long waves—from an unusual direction gave warning. Explanation: Seas and swells travel faster than the storm system itself. Reaching shore, the same swells change the familiar pattern of the surf from one wave every four to six seconds to a ten- to twelve-second rhythm. The character of the surf also changes. The gentle breathing of the sleeping ocean is replaced by waves crashing on the beach noisily. These signs were supposed to give up to several days' warning.

A falling barometer is another well-known sign, very noticeable in the tropics, where the glass ordinarily follows lazily a gentle twice-daily rhythm. But that's not an early warning; the glass may not begin to drop noticeably until twelve hours before a storm. The rapid drop may start only after shrieking winds and torrential rains are already upon you.

When the storm is within 200 nautical miles or 400 km, you may see its *bar* near the horizon. That's the nearest band of fringe clouds, perhaps 30,000 feet (10 km) high and so becoming visible at a great distance. As the storm clouds approach, the bar will get higher in the sky.

All these signs are far from unfailing. The men of South Caicos, near the southeast end of the chain of the Bahama Islands, are no strangers to hurricanes. As fishermen and sailors they have watched the skies for generations for ominous signs. One fine September day in 1945 the fishing fleet went out as usual. By nightfall fifty of the men had lost their lives.

Naval meteorologists and ship's officers are more sophisticated than simple fishermen. Yet during World War II Admiral Halsey's Third Fleet not once but twice steamed into the teeth of a typhoon.

Uncounted ships, and lives ashore, have been lost by what seemed to be the return of a storm. After the shrieking winds subsided and the sky cleared, a ship may have hoisted sail again, people ashore would go out to assess the damage and make repairs. Then the winds would hit again with full fury from the opposite direction. What really happened—as everybody should know by now—was that the *eye* of the storm had just passed. While the entire storm system may be hundreds of miles or kilometers across, its center is a circular area of insignificant winds or calms, and often of blue sky, typically a dozen miles in diameter.

From data collected, averages of the number of storms per year and for each month have been calculated for different areas. In the North Atlantic, for instance, between 1931 and 1975 the yearly average of tropical storms was 9.5, of which 5.5 reached hurricane status. Of these hurricanes an average of 1.8 reached the coasts of the United States.

But averages are misleading: In the same period up to five hurricanes struck these shores in one year; in six years not a single such storm touched them. Also, since records have been kept, there have been years without any hurricanes reported in the entire North Atlantic. And in one year there were twenty-one.

Monthly frequencies are not overly reliable either. These storms are most common between June and November, with a peak frequency in September. But they have also hit in May and December. In fact, though rarely, in any month of the year.

The "usual" tracks of such storms are even more misleading. Pilot charts show the tracks of past hurricanes for each month. There is a tendency for North Atlantic hurricanes early in the season to move west and to exit through the Caribbean. Later in the season hurricanes tend to move first somewhat north of west, and then to recurve toward the northeast, toward Bermuda and the open Atlantic.

Similar tendencies are recorded in other oceans (with the recurving in the southern hemisphere toward the southeast). Tracks and trends are generalities. They make you cheer or fret according to your temperament, when you are sweating out a storm waiting for the next advisory.

I used to compare the present storm to others while my schooner was tied with twelve lines to a thicket of mangroves. On all nearby boats the skippers did the same. When we compared notes, there were always two opinions: "It's coming our way," and "The worst is going to miss us this time." When things looked very bleak, I'd advance the eternal optimist's theory: "It's like the Ruritanian gendarmes. You are safe if they aim right at you."

For home forecasting of a storm's movement, past performance is a poor method. Hurricanes don't move on railroad tracks; many don't follow trends; nor do they maintain course and speed. One expert has classified hurricanes by their movements and has come up with some catchy names. He lists textbookers, righthookers, southdroppers, fishhookers, straightshooters and more.

Also it is little comfort to know that the eye will miss you by 50 nautical miles when 90-knot winds reach out 100 miles in your direction.

We now know that the winds in these storms invariably blow counterclockwise around the center (in the northern hemisphere), while at the same time the storm system as a whole moves forward at much slower speeds—much as the brush of a floor polisher turns rapidly, while you push the machine forward slowly. In the tropics the forward speed is typically around 10 knots. After the system recurves and gets away from the tropics, the speed usually increases to, say, 30–50 knots.

You probably have figured this out: Since the winds in tropical storms in the northern hemisphere blow counterclockwise around the center, they are Lows. Lows of extremely low central pressure. In the eye, sea-level pressure of 28 inches of mercury (about 950 mb) is common in severe hurricanes. Most of the drop in pressure is concentrated near the center of the storm, typically within 50 or 100 nautical miles. In that area the isobars will be very closely spaced, the winds unbelievably strong.

What makes hurricanes so destructive? Almost everyone has experienced wind speeds of 30–35 knots. Such winds break a few twigs, blow lids off garbage cans, and may damage a flimsy shack. But solid buildings and even small craft at sea survive them without damage. Now double that wind speed to that of a minimal hurricane. The wind pressure doesn't just double, it quadruples. Step it up to 100 knots—a common wind speed near the center of a run of the season hurricane—and you have nine times the original pressure on buildings and masts. At 130 knots—scale 3 on a scale of 5 for hurricane disaster potential—you have sixteen times the original wind pressure. Large trees will be uprooted, roofs blown off, windows and doors caved in, small buildings and mobile homes destroyed.

Here we are talking about sustained wind speeds. In between these whacking winds there will be gusts, perhaps 20 per cent higher, with pressures twenty-two times greater than in a common storm.

Add to that flying debris. A trash-can lid becomes a can opener, a ladder a battering ram. My schooner was on a marine railway for routine maintenance when hurricane warnings were hoisted. Local advice: "Stay where you are; safest place in the area." My little vessel was solidly cradled and secured to the rail bed. During the storm a sheet of plywood, torn from a building, hit two 10-by-10-inch posts that supported the railway. One rail collapsed. The schooner fell six feet, impaling herself on some pilings nearby.

Hurricane damage near shore is compounded by what is commonly called the tidal wave. It has little to do with tide. Storm surge is a better name for it. True, in bays and estuaries an approaching storm may prevent the normal tides from running out. That will maintain a state of high tide. Also if a storm surge happens to arrive at the time of especially high tides—usually a couple of days after new and full moon—the flooding will be added to an already high water level.

Add to that the effect of low barometric pressure. As the pressure over the ocean drops, the local sea level rises. At any place the sea level is in balance with all the forces that act on the water —mainly: gravity, centrifugal force due to the rotation of the earth, the attraction of moon and sun, and atmospheric pressure. Reduce the atmospheric pressure, and the sea under the Low will rise. There's another way to visualize that. High atmospheric pressure all around the Low presses down on the ocean and pushes it up where the pressure is lower, much as pressing down on a pillow raises a bump where you don't push. That effect raises the sea level about one foot for a drop of one inch of mercury (about one centimeter for a drop of one millibar). In a severe hurricane that will add several feet to the water level near the eye.

The main effect is from wind-driven seas. In a hurricane of hazard potential 3 (winds of 84–96 knots) the weather service will forecast a local storm surge of 9–12 feet (3–4 m). Since roads will be flooded hours before the arrival of the center of the storm, an early evacuation of the shore and low-lying areas will be ordered.

In the Galveston disaster of September 1900, in which six thousand people perished, the water crested 15 feet (5 m) above the high-tide mark. Hurricane Camille, in August 1969, flooded the

Louisiana and Mississippi coasts with a 24-foot (7-m) surge. Even higher surges have been reported in the Bay of Bengal.

There is no doubt about the source of the tremendous power of these storms. (The total energy in an average hurricane is estimated as the equivalent of forty hydrogen bombs detonated every second.) As you will see presently in detail, the source of all that energy is in the warm, moist air such as lies over tropical and subtropical oceans. When insufficient water vapor enters the storm, the process should stop. Over land a hurricane will lose strength rapidly and become disorganized, especially over mountainous terrain, say in passing over Cuba. Flat land, such as Florida, has much less calming effect. Hurricanes have crossed Florida from the Gulf to the Atlantic, and the other way, with virtually undiminished strength.

During such passages over land these storms cause a third calamity: floods. Safe from storm surges and the worst wind damage, inland areas such as Tennessee and Ohio are ravaged by the results of torrential rains. It is not unusual for a storm to dump 10 or 12 inches (25–30 cm) of rain in one day. That's about double what such cities of wet reputation as Seattle or Vancouver get in their rainiest month; it is also about one-fourth the total rainfall these cities get in one whole year.

Such rainfalls will cause extensive damage even when the storm is poorly organized, breaking up, with winds in the ordinary storm range.

Well into this century it was not easy to know when a hurricane was threatening. At sea there were well-established rules of behavior. The master of a vessel in a hurricane-prone area, especially in the season of their greatest frequency, would be alert to all the known advance signs. When he encountered winds or swells from an unusual direction, he would locate the center of the disturbance by Buys Ballot's law.

He would then determine if his vessel was in the "dangerous" semicircle or the "navigable" one—less dangerous would be a better description. These terms have their origin in the observed fact that winds in the northeast quadrant are usually stronger—and reach out farther—than in the southwest quadrant (in the northern hemisphere).

That's partially explained by the normal northwesterly forward
movement of the storm system. The forward speed adds to the
wind speed in the dangerous sector, subtracts from it in the
navigable one. There was more to it. The captain would heave to
—getting most or all sail off, or reducing a steamer's speed to bare
steering way to limit strains—in such a way that the wind would
blow the vessel away from the storm rather than setting her into
the storm's path. The rules—for both hemispheres—had to be
memorized by every candidate for a mate's ticket. They are still
printed in every shipboard manual.

When ships began to carry wireless equipment, they would be
warned of the existence of a traveling storm and be given the ap-
proximate current position and likely course of its center. Every
ship in hurricane waters had to report by radio any unusually
strong winds encountered. From only two such simultaneous reports in different parts of the ocean the weather office could get a
fix on the position of the storm by applying Buys Ballot's law.
From later reports it could estimate the recent course and speed
of the hurricane.

These ships' reports were vital since there are no land stations
near the area of formation of most of these storms. There just is
no land.

A breakthrough in explaining and forecasting the formation of
hurricanes came in the 1940s. G. E. Dunn, then in charge of the
Puerto Rico weather bureau, noticed that the normal trade wind
weather would regularly be interrupted by what he named *waves
in the easterlies.*

You can see the wave shape of the surface isobars in figure 27.
The line that indicates the trough of lowest pressure is *not* a
front. The air is maritime tropical ahead and astern of the trough.
And it is of the same temperature.

When such an easterly wave passes through your area you'll see
the usual puffy cumulus clouds replaced by bands of towering,
rain-bearing cumulus. The cotton-ball clouds of normal trade
wind weather reach from the dew point level to the level of the
temperature inversion, usually found at 6,000–10,000 feet (2–3
km) above the surface. That inversion normally separates the
moist surface air from dry air above. Now the inversion is wiped

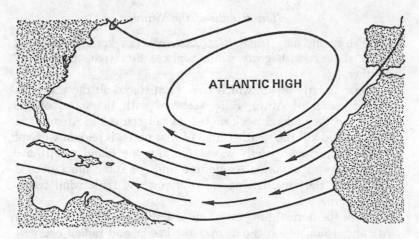

26. Normal trade wind pressure distribution over the North Atlantic. Arrows indicate air flow above the friction layer—near 3,000 feet (1,000 m).

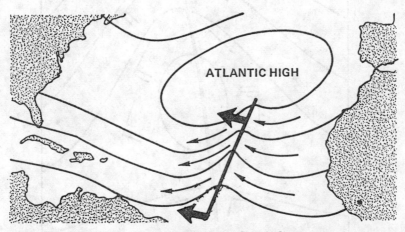

27. Easterly wave in mid-Atlantic. Heavy line indicates trough of pressure, heavy arrows motion of entire system. Light arrows show air flow above friction layer.

out. Moist air may reach to 50,000 feet (15 km). A series of
heavy showers with gusty winds replaces the serene trade wind
weather.

These easterly waves, which have been traced all the way back
to the center of Africa, drift westward with the speed of the
trades. So they take a week or two to sail across the Atlantic. In
summer and fall the weather map of that ocean is seldom without
one or more such easterly waves. On any one island you'll have
several days of abnormal cloudiness and get some much-needed
rain. Then the wave has passed over you and trade wind conditions return.

That's the normal progress of an easterly wave across the North
Atlantic. (Similar waves pass over the Pacific and Indian oceans.)
But occasionally an easterly wave will develop into a tropical

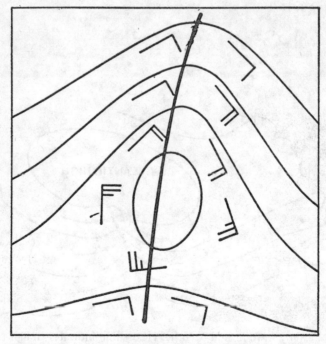

28. Easterly wave (enlarged) in which closed circulation
has formed. Note eliptical isobar and increased wind speeds
near it.

depression. That is an area of low pressure with one or more closed isobars and winds of less than 33 knots. The *tropical disturbance* of the U. S. National Weather Service is an even earlier development. It shows at least one closed isobar and only slight counterclockwise wind flow. On the weather report you'll hear, "An area of closed circulation has formed, which planes will investigate tomorrow." On the satellite picture you'd see a fuzzy, often circular, patch of cloud.

I have watched an easterly wave develop into a tropical depression. My schooner was in a well-protected anchorage in the Bahamas while a nastier than usual easterly wave seemed to sit above us. That, of course, is a personal view. The wave moved, but since it was several hundred miles wide I was having three days of intermittent heavy showers, with spurts of anchor-rattling wind. Even between these fits the wind was strong enough to make it impractical to go ashore or even visit the nearest yacht. It had turned northerly, where winds in the islands have no business blowing from in summer. On the morning of the third day the weather people announced that a tropical depression had formed. Later that day the depression had deepened into a tropical storm—the first of the season. The Hurricane Center assigned it a name and gave its co-ordinates. Just about between my masts.

What accounts for some easterly waves developing a closed circulation and the later development to a tropical storm? Here's one explanation. At about 30,000 feet (10 km) the easterly trades peter out. Above that level there are westerly winds, as in higher latitudes, carrying Highs and Lows with them. If a High happens to drift over the trough of an easterly wave, it pumps air out of it at high levels. Replacement air must flow in near the bottom. Sea-level pressure drops. The inflowing air and the Coriolis effect combine to create a vortex. When wind speeds in that whirl reach 33 knots, you get a tropical storm.

Many such storms with their thunderheads, squalls, and showers never reach hurricane intensity. They cause minimal damage and die out after a few days.

What distinguishes them from hurricanes? One attractive theory says the temperature in the center. In a young tropical storm the core is a little cooler than the surrounding air. In a hurricane it is warmer. The warmer its center the more vicious the storm. In severe hurricanes temperature differences of 10–15 degrees Fahrenheit (5–8 degrees Celsius) have been measured by planes investigating the storm and flying right through its eye at different levels.

What warms the air? A foehnlike effect. You'll recall the mechanism that causes these warm, dry, descending winds. Moist air has been forced aloft by mountains. Rising, it cools by expansion. Above the dew point level clouds form. That means water vapor is changed to water droplets. That change from the gaseous to the liquid state releases the energy originally supplied to change liquid water to steam. The release of this energy warms the air. When it descends on the other side of the mountain, it is further heated by compression as the atmospheric pressure on it increases. It arrives at the foot of the mountain warmer than it had been at the same level on the windward side. (And it has lost its moisture.)

In these storms the mechanism may be similar. All around the center moist air rises. In the eye air descends. The descending air is thrown out of the eye at low level and pulls more air—from the top—after itself. That descending air is dry; that's why there are no clouds in the eye.

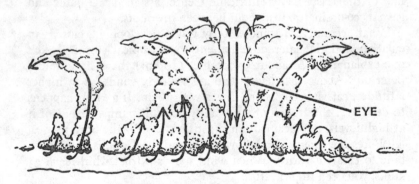

29. Cross section through part of a hurricane.

What forms the eye in the first place isn't entirely clear. You may compare it to the hollow core in the vortex of water running out of your sink. Or perhaps you may recall the ring that forms in the dishpan experiment around the center of rotation where fast-moving currents meet.

To summarize: An easterly wave does not show closed circulation. If closed circulation develops under the influence of a High in the upper atmosphere, the eye must be well organized to cause further intensification. You may hear on a weather report, "The disturbance has been investigated by aircraft and found to be poorly organized." That means the eye is very large, perhaps of odd shape instead of being circular, and possibly showing gaps.

Without a well-organized eye no tropical storm, no hurricane. When only the air near the bottom of the eye is warmer than the surrounding air, development will stop, perhaps at the lower range of tropical storm winds. When the entire core, right up to the level of the highest cloud tops, is warmer than air at the same level outside the eye, you'll get intensification to hurricane force.

You can visualize this intensification. The warmer the air in the eye, the lighter it will be, the lower the barometric pressure in the center. The lower the central pressure, the stronger the winds near the eye. The increasing winds bring more moisture per minute. The added moisture releases more heat to further warm the core.

Regardless of the fine points of the explanation, there is absolutely no doubt that the tremendous energy of these storms, the winds, and the wind-whipped seas come from one simple process: the release of heat that has been expended by the sun earlier and elsewhere to turn seawater into water vapor.

On a map of the world on which the known tracks of tropical storms had been drawn you would notice at a glance one strange fact. All the tracks start over tropical or subtropical waters, but none starts close to the equator. Explanation: In the lowest latitudes the Coriolis effect, which makes winds turn counterclockwise around Lows in the northern hemisphere and the other way in the southern, is too small to start a merry-go-round.

At latitude 5° the turning force, which is ten units in mid latitudes, drops to a little more than one unit. At latitude 15°, where many tropical storm tracks start, it is three times as strong.

If such a map were drawn for each month of the year, you would find an interesting trend. In both hemispheres the storms are most frequent when the surface temperature of the sea is the highest of the year. That's about three months after the beginning of summer in each hemisphere. It gives the correct maximum, in September for the northern hemisphere, March for the southern.

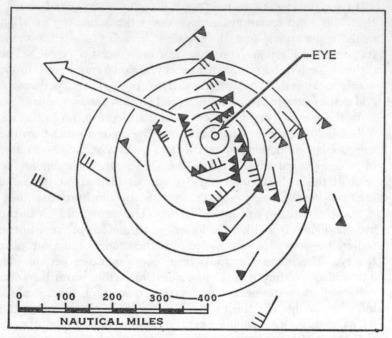

30. Isobars and winds around a hurricane in the northern hemisphere.
Large arrow shows forward movement of system. Small arrows indicate
wind direction. Each feather stands for a wind speed of 10 knots, each
flag for 50 knots.

On either side of the maximum the frequency of storms drops just
about in the manner a statistician would predict.

Can this correlation between tropical storms and surface temperature of the oceans explain the absence of such storms in the
South Atlantic? Recently two workers, Palmén and Newton,
charted the sea surface temperature in all oceans for the month of
greatest hurricane frequency. Then they plotted the principal
tracks of tropical storms on the same map. Their map shows the
storm tracks in all oceans starting in areas where the sea-water
temperature was at least 27° C (about 81° F). In the South Atlantic only a small patch of ocean normally reaches that temperature at the required latitude from the equator.

Today it is unlikely that a hurricane or typhoon would strike without warning. Their cloud pattern is unmistakable on the pictures sent routinely to earth by satellites circling the globe or hovering above it.

In the North Atlantic when a cloud pattern showing storm potential comes within range, a plane will be dispatched from Bermuda, Puerto Rico, or Florida to investigate its physical characteristics. Crammed with sophisticated weather instruments, the plane will penetrate the storm area at different levels, going repeatedly through the eye if an eye has already formed. The meteorologists aboard plot barometric pressure, temperature, humidity, wind direction, and wind speed all through the storm from near wave-top level up to the height limit of the plane.

On your radio or television set you will get only a brief summary. The location of the center—to tenths of a degree of latitude and longitude, about 6 nautical miles—central pressure, maximum wind speed, how far storm winds reach out in different directions, and whether the storm is expected to intensify within the next twelve or twenty-four hours, when another reconnaissance flight is scheduled.

From upper-air soundings by this and other planes, by ships, and at land stations the forecaster ashore predicts the direction and speed of the forward movement of the storm. It is the upper-air circulation that determines the future path of the storm.

When the "steering currents" are strong, the people at the Hurricane Center, aided by computers, are remarkably accurate in predicting positions twelve hours in advance. Typically their error is less than the diameter of the eye of the storm.

When a storm comes within range of radar (say 250 nautical miles from Puerto Rico, Miami, or New Orleans) it can be kept under constant surveillance.

Problems arise when the steering currents are weak. The storm will move erratically, now this way now that, and at varying speeds including no speed at all. A crucial point in forecasting is the place (and the time) where the storm will recurve. To shore dwellers it makes all the difference. A storm that had been aiming at you from the southeast won't bother you much if it recurves well offshore toward the northeast.

Small but intense storms—they come in all combinations of ferocity and size (say from 60 to 1,000 nautical miles in diameter)—

pose another problem. Here is a textbook example: Indications are that such a small storm in the next twenty-four hours will parallel the coasts of Georgia and the Carolinas, far enough offshore to cause no more than 30-knot winds at the coast. But what if the upper-air High, supposed to keep the storm offshore, moves somewhat slower? Then these three states would get the full brunt of the 120-knot winds near the center.

Aren't you glad you don't have to forecast, but just to listen to the latest advisories, follow instructions, and . . . pray?

14

Unusual Winds: Tornadoes

The highest winds on the surface of the earth occur in tornadoes. Speeds of 300 knots and more have been estimated. In a recent study of one year's crop of tornadoes in the United States, nine out of ten showed wind speeds of up to 140 knots, comparable to winds in a severe hurricane. One out of every hundred of the studied tornadoes was calculated to have had speeds of between 180 and 226 knots.

Western man, who didn't learn about hurricanes until the discovery of America, has known about tornadoes for thousands of years. They are the whirlwinds of the Bible, the cyclones of literature. These names, tornado, and the midwestern twister, imply rotation.

Hurricanes, by whatever local name, are revolving storms. But it takes several observations at distant points to deduce the pattern of circulation. In a tornado you *see* rotating debris, which may have been seconds earlier a house. On a plowed field a tornado leaves swirl marks as if a giant had used a rotary sander clumsily.

Except in pictures taken from satellites you never see a whole hurricane. Everybody within miles sees the whole of a tornado: a violently rotating column of air between the ground and the base of a thundercloud. You don't actually see the air, of course, but water droplets—as in a cloud—and junk whirling about.

The tornado may take the shape of a long narrow funnel, a column, an elephant's trunk, or a writhing snake. And it may change shape before your eyes from one minute to the next. It may be almost straight up and down, or slant at just about any angle to the horizon.

Like a hurricane, the rotating system of high-speed winds moves
forward at much lower speed. Typically it advances at 30–40 miles
per hour (40–65 km/h). So, if you saw a tornado bearing down on
you, you might outrun it in an automobile even on a country
road.

While a hurricane lasts for days and travels thousands of miles
(kilometers), a typical tornado lasts only for minutes. In that time
it travels less than 10 miles (16 km). But one out of a hundred
tornadoes may last an hour or more, and devastate a strip 30–100
miles (50–160 km) long. A hurricane's destruction in such a strip
would be unbroken. A tornado may lift off the ground, spare a
few city blocks, and then touch down again, flattening more
houses.

The width of the path of destruction of a hurricane may be
hundreds of miles (kilometers); the path of a typical tornado is
less than 500 feet (150 m) wide. But the worst tornadoes have
razed strips three to nine times as wide.

Air pressure in tornadoes, as in the center of hurricanes, is ab-
normally low. Tornadoes have happened to pass directly over
barographs. From such recordings and studies of the effect on
buildings of known strength, experts put the pressure drop at up
to 4 inches of mercury (135 mb). That gives sea-level pressures
lower than the lowest accepted reading in the eye of a hurricane.

In a hurricane that passes over you the pressure drop is spread
over several hours. In a tornado the drop takes place in an instant.
The pressure on the outside of a window 40 inches (1 m)
square would suddenly be 1½ tons less than on the inside. No
wonder roofs blow off, barns explode. Once airborne, the remains
of the roof or barn are lifted by updrafts, whirled about by the revolving winds, and carried forward with the funnel cloud.

Don't think of tornadoes as severe, small, short-lived hurricanes.
Hurricanes *always* form over water in or near the tropics. Tornadoes spring up regularly over land, and in any latitude. They
have been reported over every continent, and in every state in the
United States, even Alaska.

Hurricanes must turn counterclockwise (in the northern hemisphere). Some tornadoes turn the other way.

Tornadoes are always associated with severe thunderstorms.
(Officially a thunderstorm becomes severe when wind speeds ex-

ceed 50 knots on the ground—or when it unleashes hail.) Hurricanes often generate thunderstorms. Such thunderstorms may reach severe levels and then spawn tornadoes. Hurricane Beulah, in 1967, raised sixty-nine of them over Texas.

Hurricanes develop as single units, rarely in pairs; only at long intervals will more than two related hurricanes be on a daily weather map. Tornadoes regularly come in families. Large families.

On Palm Sunday of 1965 some forty tornadoes killed almost as many people. On April 3, 1974—the day of the Xenia disaster—148 separate twisters caused 300 deaths, 5,000 injuries, and many hundred millions of dollars' property damage between Decatur, Alabama, and Windsor, Ontario. Two days earlier, for a dress rehearsal, nature had arranged for twenty tornadoes in ten states.

With such disasters you can imagine that much research into causes and prediction, and work on better warning systems is going on. Especially in the United States, the undisputed record holder for the yearly number of tornadoes. The annual average is about 850. The number has been increasing recently, partly due to more sophisticated spotting techniques. But better observation cannot account for the jump to 1,108 tornadoes in 1973.

In the United States tornadoes occur most often east of the Rockies, especially in the Mississippi drainage basin.

Tornadoes have been recorded in every month, but they are most frequent in late spring and early summer. In Oklahoma and Kansas, two of the busiest twister states, three out of four tornadoes strike in April, May, and June. Early in the season twisters are more common in the states bordering the Gulf of Mexico; later they work their way toward the Canadian border.

Four out of five tornadoes strike between noon and midnight. The busiest time of day is 2:00–9:00 P.M., when two out of three hit.

Most often they move from southwest to northeast, like other bad weather. Occasionally they stall, and sometimes even double back.

Such statistics are little comfort if in an area of few reported tornadoes your house is unroofed in October, after midnight, by a twister moving from the northwest.

The public has demanded prediction of tornadoes from the

weather office service from its very beginning, more than a hundred years ago. But meteorologists then knew virtually nothing about the conditions in the atmosphere above the level of their ground-based instruments. No theory had been formulated on which to base the forecast of a tornado at a given place and time.

Local forecasters were expressly forbidden to use the word tornado in a forecast. The closest they'd come: "Conditions in western Kansas are favorable for severe local storms this afternoon."

We now have tornado data collected over many years and at many places, vastly more surface weather observations, upper-air soundings every few hours all over the country, and more sophisticated weather instruments. So how does the forecast read today? "Conditions in western Kansas are favorable for severe local storms this afternoon."

When conditions seem critical in one area, the Weather Service will issue a tornado-watch bulletin one to several hours in advance of the danger. It means: Look out for funnel clouds; keep your radio or television set tuned to a local station for further more precise information. Tornadoes materialize in only about one out of three such watches.

Under what conditions will the weatherman expect likely tornado formation? You already have one clue. Tornadoes are always associated with thunderstorms. Not the local variety that forms where heating of the surface makes air rise until cumulus clouds grow to great height. Tornado formation is to be expected along a system of many thunderstorms, a squall line.

Such a squall line forms—outside regular tornado areas, and often in winter—when an advancing cold front pushes warm, moist surface air upstairs.

In a typical tornado-threatening situation in the United States the warm air is marine tropical air flowing from the south. It comes from the Gulf of Mexico and is driven by the circulation around a High over the east coast or the Atlantic. That's a common pattern in spring and summer over the Gulf states and the Mississippi basin. To create the danger of severe thunderstorms, something else is needed. Above the warm layer, cold air must be flowing at high velocity from the southwest or west. It may be driven by a bight in a jet stream strong enough to reach down to, say, the 6,000-foot (2,000-m) level. (The normal seasonal migration of the polar jet toward the north would explain the shift of maximum tornado activity from the Gulf states toward Canada.)

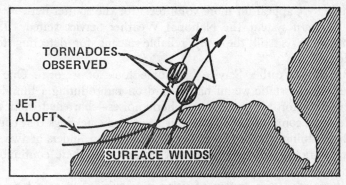

31. Tornado situation

Now all it needs to create a series of thunderstorms along a narrow zone is some lifting mechanism. Perhaps the daily warming cycle of the ground will do it. (That certainly explains the observed frequency of *local* thunderstorms in the afternoon, when the ground is warmest.)

Normally the warm air will rise until it loses buoyancy, having been cooled by its own expansion. A few very active cells will reach higher than others. When they encounter colder, heavier air aloft, they become buoyant again and take off once more. More warm air rises through these "chimneys." You can see how a number of cells forming along one line—the edge of the polar jet stream—will form a squall line hundreds of miles long.

It is along the southern edge of such a squall line that tornadoes sometimes form. You may see bag-shaped clouds hanging from the lowest layer of thunderclouds. Some of these bags may stretch to take the shape of a funnel. But until this funnel reaches all the way to the ground it's officially still not a tornado, but a funnel cloud.

When someone sees a funnel cloud that reaches close to the ground—you can't tell from a distance whether it touches the ground—he may phone the sheriff. The sheriff calls the weather office, which will immediately have a tornado warning broadcast. Local systems of volunteers and warnings—by church bells and fire-house sirens—have been used in the tornado belt for a long time. Even now most warnings by the weather office are based on tornado sightings by outsiders, often law officers or firemen.

In a 1975 appeal for more volunteers for the spotter network of the *Skywarn* system, the National Weather Service stated, "The human eye is still the only reliable means for detecting tornadoes."

But the Weather Service has some tools of its own. One is based on the static we all have heard on radio during a thunderstorm. In a tornado these atmospheric noises—shortened: sferics— are almost continuous and without the sharp cracklings that come with lightning strokes. By using radio direction finders at two or more stations, one can pinpoint the source of these continuous sferics and follow their path.

I have read of a system of using a television set as a tornado warning device, or more precisely as a tornado-caused-sferics receiver. But until the system has been checked by unbiased tests, I'd rather not talk about the technique. Someone may use these instructions when he should have the set tuned to warning bulletins . . . and get clobbered by a tornado.

In the 1950s it was discovered that many tornadoes form along a line where a sensitive barometer would indicate a sudden increase in atmospheric pressure. One hundred automatic alarms were installed in tornado country—25–30 miles (40–50 km) apart —to warn the nearest weather office staff when such a pressure jump occurred. Unfortunately not all tornadoes trip the alarm.

The warm, moist air penetrating into the cold level forms water drops and hailstones that show clearly on radar. In the mass of echoes a tornado usually cannot be distinguished. But once a tornado has been located—say by a cruising patrol car—the weather people can track the movement of the thunderstorm in which that tornado is embedded and warn communities in its path.

Sometimes an echo shaped like a letter S or a figure 6 appears among the other echoes on the radar screen. This "hook" is not the tornado itself but a danger signal: Tornado forming here. Hooks have been seen half an hour before a tornado was observed. During the tornado outbreak that caused the Xenia disaster, the Cincinnati radar at one time showed four such hooks within 90 miles (140 km) from the station.

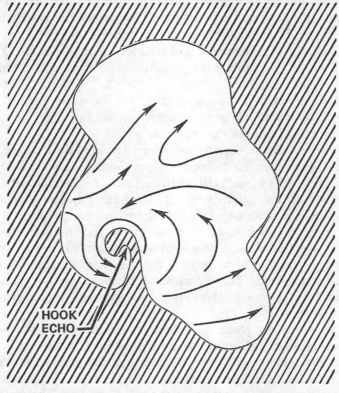

HOOK
ECHO

32. Air flow in tornado-bearing thunderstorm

A more sophisticated radar system—pulsed Doppler radar—may hold the key for the near future. It measures the movement of raindrops and hailstones toward and away from the observer. It works on the principle, named after the Austrian physicist Christian Johann Doppler, we have all observed: The pitch of a siren changes when it comes toward us and when it moves away. The faster the car carrying the siren travels, the greater the change in pitch. The electromagnetic waves sent out by the radar set and reflected by the hailstones and raindrops act in similar fashion.

Such a system can be made fully automatic, and unlike a human radar observer it works without getting tired of staring at the screen. When it observes the signature of a tornado—nearby particles moving in opposite directions at high speed—it rings an alarm. It also gives the bearing and distance of the twister from the station. By tracking it, one can estimate its future path.

The range of such a radar is of the order of 125 miles (200 km). So it would take quite a few installations to cover only the most tornado-prone states.

If the effect of a tornado reaches into the upper parts of the parent thunderstorm, as one expert believes, a single stationary satellite could monitor the entire country.

When a tornado warning for an area has been broadcast, everyone seeks shelter. First choice: a specially constructed structure, still called a "cyclone" cellar although the weather people have tried for decades to eradicate that word as applied to tornadoes. Scare hole, another popular name, describes what people in it do. It's a simple thing to build: a root-cellar-type structure covered with a few feet of soil, with a solid door and some means for ventilation. I have read a statement that no one has ever been killed in a tornado shelter. That was written a few years ago but probably is still true. No wonder there are so many of them in rural areas in tornado alley.

The next best place, according to experts, is the southwest corner of a cellar. Corner because it's strongest; southwest in the hope the tornado will come from that direction and blow your house, should it collapse, away from you. If nothing better is available, follow your instinct and crawl under the bed. The mattress may buffer the shock of the collapsing ceiling.

What do people do in a cyclone shelter, besides praying and worrying? Talk about tornadoes, of course.

You may hear discussions of the noise that often makes a person look up and first *see* the twister. Agreement on the sound is not likely. Some describe it as "inside a swarm of bees," others as an express train rolling over you in a tunnel, others as the take-off of a whole fleet of jet planes.

Then come memories of tornadoes past, experienced or heard about. A wheat straw imbedded six inches in an oak . . . a plank several feet long driven straight into another tree, and supporting the weight of a man like a diving board . . . a 6-by-8-inch (15-by-20-cm) timber driven 4 feet (120 cm) into hard soil . . . a mile-long barbed-wire fence in Kansas, with all posts pulled out, rolled up into one neat roll.

A gasoline truck and several cars overturned inside a road tunnel in Texas . . . a pair of trousers with a wallet containing $95 found 39 miles (62 km) away . . . a railroad locomotive picked up, and set down—facing the other way—neatly on the other track . . . a house in Oklahoma picked up, turned ninety degrees, set back down on its own foundations and still inhabited, sideways to the road, decades later . . . wells, and even streams sucked dry . . . chickens stripped of all their feathers. (Was that the force of pretornado air trapped in the hollow quills pushing them out? If so, how about a vacuum chicken-plucking machine?)

A sheriff in Alabama, sheltering face down in a ditch, carried some 200 yards (meters) . . . a fellow blown over the tree tops; his friend, trying to hold him, sailing in a slightly different direction over Texas, with both landing after a 200-foot (60-m) trip—unharmed . . . a schoolhouse with teacher and sixteen pupils carried 150 yards (meters) . . . a man finding his house gone but his wife and children unharmed amid the foundations; of all the house and furnishings only one piece remaining: a wobbly floor lamp.

A gentleman from Iowa who has been attacked by twisters three times—twice in Iowa, once in North Dakota—says, "Somebody's got it in for me. It's getting closer every time." He has now moved to southern Florida, one of the statistically safer areas, and is awaiting developments.

I wish I could explain how a tornado forms on a family of thunderstorms or a squall line. There is still no generally accepted theory.

Perhaps it has to wait until someone measures conditions inside a tornado and at different levels. Better, in many tornadoes. Balloons haven't a chance. Manned planes are out of the question. Unmanned drones would probably disintegrate before they could take useful measurements. Could instrumented rockets be fired through a twister, perhaps on a spiraling trajectory? Would the electricity in the tornado interfere with the rockets' operation and measurements? Nobody knows.

There is, no question about it, a lot of electricity in and around tornadoes. One man actually looked up into the funnel of a twister, and reported continuous sheets of lightning in there. At night some tornadoes have been seen to glow as if lit from the inside like Chinese lanterns, the light strong enough to penetrate the cloud of water vapor and dust.

So it is not surprising that some researchers believe that tornadoes are formed and maintained by electrical phenomena. They have proved mathematically that the available electric energy is of about the right magnitude to account for the observed phenomena. But some tornadoes, to quote another researcher in the field, "do not exhibit any unusual electrical characteristics."

Here's another theory. In the early stages of formation you have a rotating *updraft*. City dwellers have seen such updrafts at the base of tall buildings whirling papers and dust skyward; farmers see them over bare dry soil; they are common over desert sands: dust devils. In a tornado the water vapor at higher levels turns into water drops and perhaps ice crystals. They grow until they become raindrops (or perhaps hailstones), which begin to fall causing *downdrafts*. These downdrafts rapidly accelerate while continuing to rotate. The twisting downdrafts lead to the formation of a tornado.

Perhaps so. But I'm sure you have a lot of questions to ask about that. I certainly have one: If that's the mechanism, why don't tornadoes form more often? Even in massive outbreaks only one in ten thunderstorms spawns a twister, and each thunderstorm consists of several visible updrafts.

The answer has perhaps been found in a series of experiments recently reported from the North Dakota State University at Fargo. Three men, Gillies, Withnell, and Glass, built what they modestly called "an apparatus to produce tornado-like vortices in the laboratory." You and I might call it a tornado box.

The box, open at the top, seems necessary to keep outside drafts away from the experiment. It has to be rather large—3 feet (90 cm) in the Fargo setup—to keep the air streams used to produce a tornado from bouncing off the walls and spoiling the effect.

To make the tornado visible, the Fargo group bubbled air first through hydrochloric acid, then through ammonium hydroxide. That formed an ammonium chloride fog more than one inch (3 cm) deep on the bottom of the box. Dry ice would probably work too.

At first they used three nozzles, each mounted with lab clamps on a stand. Each nozzle could be moved about in the box, raised or lowered, and aimed at any angle. One nozzle, pointed straight down and blowing cooled air was to simulate the downdraft required by the theory. The two other nozzles produced horizontal air streams corresponding to the winds aloft.

The experimenters shifted and turned these nozzles, and twisted valves to control air speed. Eventually they produced miniature tornadoes. But they lasted at most one second.

They then did away with the downdraft and, after more trial and error, found that two horizontal air streams alone could create laboratory tornadoes when the angle between the streams was 65 degrees. And only then.

33. Tornado box. Air streams at 65-degree angle. The left blower is tilted to 6 degrees below the horizontal.

How long the tornado in the box lasted depended very little on the velocity of the "winds," but was greatest when one of the nozzles was depressed 6 degrees below the horizontal plane. With that setup the vortex in the box would last up to twenty seconds.

The vortices in the box had the classic shapes of tornadoes in the field: funnels, columns, elephant trunks, snakes. . . . When one of these shapes became unstable, it would lift from the ground, just as tornadoes do in nature.

Multiple tornadoes were commonly produced in the box, but their lifetimes never exceeded eight seconds. Four out of five tornadoes in the box turned counterclockwise. That's the same ratio found by studying damage in real tornadoes.

This box experiment, and all other laboratory vortex experiments, prove nothing about tornadoes, of course. But the critical angle of the meeting airstreams may explain why tornadoes are not more common when all the other conditions for their formation are present.

In the Fargo experiment no provision for an updraft was made. Before long someone may repeat the experiment with local heating at the bottom of the box (which was masonite in Fargo). Will he produce taller vortices than the ones in Fargo—6 inches (15 cm)? Longer-lasting ones?

A waterspout is a tornado over water. Contrary to appearance—and common belief—waterspouts are *not* made of water lifted from the surface. I have seen proof of that several times: They invariably *dipped down* from a cloud, and looked exactly the same before they touched the surface as after. Also a waterspout can't possibly support the weight of a column of water, say, 3,000 feet (1,000 m) high. The pressure drop is probably of the same magnitude as measured in some tornadoes. Say 4 inches of mercury. That suction would raise water all of 55 inches (138 cm).

Some experts hold that waterspouts are less violent than twisters that form over land. Is that due to the updrafts that trigger them being weaker over water, where surface temperatures are more uniform than over land?

Waterspouts are not merely seagoing dust devils. They have been seen to go ashore and act in every way like other tornadoes, overturning mobile homes and all the rest. On the other hand, tornadoes have been seen crossing Chesapeake Bay, changing to waterspouts, and changing back to tornadoes over the Eastern

Shore. Tornadoes have also been observed crossing the Great Lakes, and resuming tornado status on the far shore.

There is another proof of their changing personality. Tornadoes have deposited over land schools of fish—fresh and salt-water species—not just pondloads of frogs.

Waterspouts, like tornadoes, come in groups. One scary day in the Bahamas I counted a dozen in less than two hours. They moved slowly, but any one of them could have overtaken my little sailboat. Most of these monsters kept their distance, but two came close enough for me to see the circle of disturbed water around their base. I'd describe their noise as a lot of steam engines popping their safety valves all at the same time.

There is a belief among sailors that waterspouts can be broken up by gunfire. The logs of many a man-of-war and armed merchant vessel report the captain ordering the gun crews to fire. If the threatening waterspout withdrew into the clouds, that was proof of success. (It might have done so anyway.) If a waterspout, after being vexed by gunfire, demolished a sailing vessel, there was no log and no survivors to report the failure.

So the belief survived into this century. Here is a description from Captain Voss, the second man to sail a small craft around the world, whom you met earlier in the doldrums in *Tilikum*, the modified Indian dugout. Two days before making Sydney, Australia, he writes:

. . . the wind had died down and the sea became quite calm. Two hours later the sky was as clear as crystal, with the exception of a very heavy cloud rising from the southwest. I watched this as it grew larger and larger. In a little while, when it rose to about forty-five degrees above the horizon, it looked like a huge arch supported on the bosom of the ocean, one abutment in the southwest and the other in the southeast, and it certainly appeared as if I was getting into another heavy gale. I therefore secured all my sails and prepared for the storm; but the cloud rose no higher, and while I was looking at it I saw what appeared to be a long, sharp point forming underneath the center of the span, which was gradually approached by a similar point rising out of the ocean, and as soon as the two points met they formed a large waterspout.

I at once made a dive down into my cabin to get my rifle on deck, which did not take longer than half a minute, and by the time I was on deck again there were two. Then, one after the other they formed until, in a very short time, there were six, the nearest at the very most, one mile from me; but there they stopped, and owing to the perfect calm I could hear the water rushing up in the cloud, which sounded something like a distant waterfall.

Shortly afterwards one of the spouts broke; then another; then another would rise; and so they kept on rising and falling, one after the other, for about three hours. The cloud got larger and larger till six o'clock, when the last spout dropped.

I may mention here that I had sailed across the South Pacific several times, and on different occasions I have seen waterspouts, but never, before or since, have I witnessed spouts of the same nature. All other waterspouts I have seen moved more or less in a slanting position, while those in question were all perfectly vertical.

During the afternoon, from about three till six o'clock, there must have been at least thirty spouts that I saw from my boat, and the nearest at any time I should judge was about a mile distant. I fired several shots at the spouts, and one of them broke shortly after I fired, but whether it broke from the effects of the vibration of the shot or from natural consequences I cannot say. I have been told by ship-masters who have had experience with waterspouts that they will break every time from the vibration of a gunshot, if it is discharged within two hundred yards. I, however, was well pleased that they kept where they were, as, had they come near my vessel, and I had been unable to break them with my gun, the *Tilikum* and I might still be sailing in the sky.

At six o'clock the bank that had up to then formed a

large arch, and by the looks of it had imbibed from the ocean thousands upon thousands of tons of water, broke up and covered the sky with dark and threatening clouds. At the same time the weather still kept calm, but I heard light thunder; then a flash of lightning was followed by a loud peal of thunder, and I then experienced a very severe thunderstorm. There was no wind with it, but occasionally very heavy rain squalls. The lightning was apparently very near my boat, for it would make the dark and cloudy night bright as day. I knew I was absolutely unable to prevent the lightning from striking my boat, so went below and laid down in my bunk to await further developments.

15

Forecasting the Wind: Tools

I mention the wind in the title of this chapter to make my editor happy. I want her to know that I haven't forgotten that this book is about wind. But if you have read this far, you'll know that wind and weather are inseparable. Weather systems cause winds, and other winds move the weather systems. So this chapter will really have to deal with forecasting weather.

Once upon a time there must have been a meteorologist, probably a very young meteorologist, who had this thought: "If we knew the state of the atmosphere all over the world at one instant, and knew all the laws that govern the processes in the atmosphere, we could predict the weather everywhere and as far into the future as we liked."

A similar thought had been expressed earlier by an astronomer. And astronomers now can indeed predict the exact position of sun, earth and moon—and from that eclipses of the sun and moon —for centuries ahead. They can just as easily calculate backward, and date to the hour eclipses reported in historical records. They can also predict the position of the planets and their moons as accurately as anyone could wish.

Why then can meteorologists *not* predict the weather accurately for next weekend?

ONE: We never know the state of the atmosphere all over the world. There are only scattered observations over the oceans, hardly any over the Arctic and Antarctic. In many parts of the world surface observations of even inhabited land are sparse. The atmosphere above the surface is measured at only about five hundred places in the entire world.

TWO: Our optimistic young meteorologist probably hoped that the laws would not only become known, but that they would be simple.

The basic equations have been known since 1920. But they are not simple. Given a set of observations, a fully staffed weather office would take twelve hours to arrive at a six-hour forecast. "That was before electronic computers," you say. True, but the computers still have not caught up. Example: Upper air observations are taken and reported at seven levels. To come up with a forecast in a usefully short time, the computer is fed only a few of these levels, and can only be given simplified equations.

THREE: The observations are not exact and small local effects cannot be dealt with adequately yet.

What is the combined effect of these difficulties? Say you have a 90 per cent chance of being correct when you project present conditions one hour into the future. You then project your projection another hour into the future. That's how computers operate. Your chance of being right is now down to 81 per cent. After six steps your chances would be 48 per cent.

Suppose, for example, you were able to forecast rain within the next hour correctly ninety times in a hundred forecasts. Using the step-by-step method, you'd forecast rain correctly six hours in advance with an accuracy of forty-eight times in a hundred. If you flipped a coin, you'd expect to be right fifty times in a hundred on the average.

Obviously the U. S. National Weather Service and the weather services of other countries do much better than that. They fairly well predict the next few stages in the self-perpetuating chaos that is the earth's atmosphere.

The history of the United States National Weather Service makes interesting reading.

As in other parts of the world, some people in the United States had been keeping systematic records of their local weather conditions. The oldest surviving record in colonial America goes back to 1644 and Rev. John Campinius in Delaware. In Charleston the weather has been recorded, without interruption, since 1670. Chief Justice of Massachusetts Paul Bradley left records for Boston for the years 1738–50, and Professor John Winthrop of Harvard for 1742–78.

The earliest co-ordinated effort for collecting data over a large area was started in 1780 by the Meteorological Society of the Palatinate. That society issued calibrated rain gauges and collected data from observers in Germany, Austria, and Switzerland. It published them every year until 1792.

In the United States Dr. James Tilton, Surgeon General of the Army, in 1812 ordered all army hospitals to keep records of the weather. Why the surgeon general? He wanted to test his theory of the connection between health and weather. That was the first federally funded weather service.

The directive wasn't popular in the field, and the support from Washington was poor. It was, for instance, not until 1836 that all stations had been supplied with rain gauges. The majority of stations kept no record of barometric pressure and dew point.

Before the introduction of the telegraph in the 1840s, these and other efforts—for example that by the Board of Regents of New York University, and the Franklin Institute—yielded not weather reports but what we would call climatological records. When all stations had sent in their monthly sheet, you could calculate the rainfall for the months, mean temperature, maximum and minimum temperature and so forth.

In 1849 Professor Joseph Henry, the first director of the Smithsonian Institution, set up an extensive network of weather observations with Western Union. The Smithsonian supplied the instruments. The telegraph operators read the instruments—all at the same times of day—and transmitted some of the data by telegraph to Washington, with the rest to follow in monthly summaries.

In the first year the Smithsonian had 150 observers. By 1854 the network had spread to thirty-one states with a couple of stations in Canada. That was more than the budget of the Smithsonian could stand; only a small number of observers were furnished a complete set of weather instruments.

From the telegraphed data Professor Henry prepared synoptic—meaning seen at the same time—maps of weather conditions across the land. He published these maps daily until the Civil War interrupted the service.

From such weather maps one could attempt to forecast the weather. You didn't have to be a genius to predict misery for New

York City tomorrow when today's map showed rain and sleet from Ontario to Tennessee. All you had to know was the fact that weather generally travels eastward or, as Benjamin Franklin had found a century earlier, more likely northeastward.

Some savvy individuals became weather forecasters. The manager of a shipping company used the Washington weather maps to forecast the weather along the eastern seaboard, an ideal forecasting situation. A Mr. Merriam, dubbed "the Sage of Brooklyn Heights," predicted the weather in the newspapers. He was no sage, just an astute cribber of other people's data.

As every student of the Civil War knows, the weather was an enemy of the Union forces. A government forecasting service might have come into being under President Lincoln in 1863.

Unfortunately a Mr. Capen, who had asked the president for a favorable reference to the War Department, had predicted, "No rain until April 30 or May 1." On April 28 Lincoln wrote in the margin of Capen's letter, "It is raining now and has been for ten hours." Capen had tried something we still can't do well. He had made a five-day prediction.

After the war Professor Henry requested $50,000 from Congress to renew the Smithsonian program. Despite a strong endorsement from the Commissioner of Agriculture, Congress turned him down.

For the first time in the history of man, scientists had the tools to predict the weather rationally. Then, as now, they were aware of the work done in other countries. For example, in Great Britain, where collection of weather observations by telegraph had started in the same year as the Smithsonian program. Or in France, where Leverrier published daily weather maps and forecasts.

All that was needed was someone to finance a practical scientist. Such a scientist was Cleveland Abbe, Sr., director of the astronomical observatory in Cincinnati. He persuaded the local Chamber of Commerce to underwrite a program. Western Union again supplied the telegraph service. Abbe was sure he could get volunteer observers to co-operate. On September 1, 1869, the opening day of his forecasting service, he received exactly two reports. Undaunted, he issued a forecast, which he called "probabilities": "Easterly and southeasterly winds." Within a year thirty stations supplied reports. But when he tried to extend the service to include all of the Great Lakes, the Chicago Board of Trade would not underwrite the added cost.

Increase A. Lapham had a state-supported program going in Wisconsin. He too tried to expand his service to cover the Great Lakes. To show how such a service could save lives and cargoes, he proved how the devastating storm of 1859 could have been predicted. The *Chicago Tribune* editorialized against the expert "who took ten years to forecast a storm."

Then Lapham got the ear of his congressman, H. E. Paine of Wisconsin. Paine had been a student of Elias Loomis, who lectured and wrote on forecasting from synoptic weather maps. Paine's legislative aim: a national weather service.

His bill, with the support of the New York Chamber of Commerce and the expert endorsement of Matthew Maury and professors Henry and Loomis, passed and was signed by President Ulysses S. Grant.

There had been hot arguments over who would control the service, civilians or the Army. Typical arguments: Army people are no more qualified than civilian telegraph operators; but military manpower is cheaper. The Army won. The Signal Service—since 1866 consisting of one chief (Colonel A. J. Meyer), six officers, and one hundred noncommissioned officers—got the job in February 1870. Its main qualification: telegraph lines strung during the Civil War.

On November 8 Colonel Meyer requested Lapham to take charge of the Great Lakes area (at a salary of $167 a month). That day Lapham issued the first report of the first national weather service in the U.S.:

> High winds all day yesterday at Cheyenne and Omaha; a very high wind this morning at Omaha; barometer falling with high winds at Chicago and Milwaukee today; barometer falling and thermometer rising at Chicago, Detroit, Cleveland, Buffalo and Rochester; high winds probable along the lakes.

In December Abbe left Cincinnati for Washington to become assistant to the Chief Signal Officer. After a month of practice forecasts, he began to issue three daily forecasts in February 1871. Here is the one of February 21:

> Synopsis for the past 24 hours: The barometric pressure has diminished in the southern and Gulf states; has remained nearly stationary on the Lakes; a decided diminution has appeared unannounced in Missouri, accompanied with a rapid rise in the thermometer which is felt as far east as Cincinnati; the barometer in Missouri is about $\frac{4}{10}$ of an inch lower than on Erie and on the Gulf. Fresh north and west winds are prevailing in the north; southerly winds in the south.
>
> Probabilities: It is probable the low pressure in Missouri will make itself felt decidedly tomorrow with northerly winds and clouds on the Lakes and brisk southerly winds on the Gulf.

In that year the meteorological service had sixty stations, a total staff of 233, and an appropriation from Congress of $15,000 (the pay for military personnel coming from Army funds). Each station was equipped with barometer, thermometer, hygrometer, anemometer and wind vane, nonrecording rain gauge, clock, toolbox, and pads of forms. The stations reported by telegraph three times a day to Washington, where all forecasts were made. The forecaster was on a tight schedule: forty-nine minutes from the receipt of the last telegram. His reference: Loomis, *Treatise on Meteorology*.

The forecasts were sent by telegraph to railroad depots and Signal Service stations. There they were put on postcards, and two thousand post offices around the country had them five hours after the midnight prediction. Associated Press distributed the forecasts by telegraph to its member newspapers.

Relations with Congress were always difficult. There were constituents who objected to weather forecasting on principle. "The weather is God's business; men should not try to outguess Him." At budget debates one congressman was sure to bring up a man in his state who predicted the weather better than the Service, using say a sourwood stick. Spectacular goofs would be read into the *Congressional Record*. "The forecast for New York City had been

for fair and warmer. We got a traffic-snarling snow fall. The Third
Avenue cars moved with difficulty even with *four* horses." "For
the inauguration of President Taft the forecast had been for
colder and clear; instead a snowstorm descended on Washington."
"And why is there no station in my district?" (Congressional pressure had an office opened in Minneapolis when St. Paul had had
one for ten years.) "The Fort Meyer training center is a luxury."
Funds for research? "A waste of money."

In the summer of 1881 Captain Henry W. Howgate was
arrested for embezzling $40,000 by means of phony vouchers. By
the time the indictment was drawn up, the amount had grown to
$90,000. The true sum is not known. But according to the *New-
York Tribune,* the chief told a House committee that the total,
spread over several years, was "possibly $237,000." Two days after
his arrest Howgate was released on bond of $30,000. In October
he forfeited his bond and was jailed. In April he was allowed to go
home with a guard to visit his daughter on spring break from
Vassar.

He gave the guard the slip. A $500 reward was offered. It went
unclaimed for twelve years.

After the embezzlement Congress reduced the budget from
$375,000 to $312,000. The Army closed eighteen stations.

Other complaints reached Congress. Blacks were not employed.
Promotions for noncommissioned officers were impossibly difficult. And why did weather service personnel have to have saber
practice? The Army was unhappy about the salaries of the
weather service people coming out of its funds.

In 1891 responsibility for the national weather service passed to
the Department of Agriculture. Many of the former employees
stayed on. The name was changed to U. S. Weather Bureau.
Later it went to Commerce. Now the name is U. S. National
Weather Service, and it's a branch of the National Oceanic and
Atmospheric Administration in the Department of Commerce.

Perhaps another approach to the history of forecasting would
be more interesting. How did inventions and technological advances help in predicting wind and weather?

It was obvious, at least since Franklin's discovery of the travel
of storms, that scientific forecasting would have to be based on

observations upstream in the atmosphere, just as flood warnings on a river have to be based on observations upriver.

Mid-latitude storm systems typically travel several hundred miles (kilometers) in one day. As long as messages traveled at the speed of a horse, the storms would outrun the message.

The telegraph made collecting upstream observations practical. (The railways, which might have outrun the weather, never were in the race. At first they didn't move much faster than horses. And the network of telegraph lines grew much faster than the rail system.)

Wireless telegraphy added thousands of observers in badly needed places, the oceans of the world. In the years just before World War I not only all naval vessels and passenger liners but most freighters carried transmitters. A system of shipboard voluntary observers began that continues to this day. Every day, at specified times, ships all over the world send their observations to the weather services of all seafaring nations.

Teletypewriters came into use after 1928. Now every airport weather office got forecasts and reports on conditions at other airports within minutes.

Almost at the same time, facsimile printers became practical. (I peeled my first wet and blurry weather map off the cylinder of a home-built facsimile printer fed by an ordinary radio set in 1927.) Now you could show a weather map, or a forecast map, drawn in Washington a few minutes before, to a pilot about to take off from San Francisco.

After World War II radar, invented to locate enemy planes at night or above the clouds, joined the tools of the meteorologist. You have read how radar detects squall lines and tornadoes possibly embedded in them. And how radar tracks hurricanes. But most of the time Weather Service radars just locate showers.

A modern refinement lets the operator measure drop size in these showers. From that he can estimate the rate of rainfall. A certain echo translates into 0.1 inch of rain per hour, another 0.2 inch and so on. Every point in the sky over the eastern and central United States is now covered by weather radar. The blank areas in the coverage over the western states are scheduled to be filled in in the next few years.

You can see radar images of showers on some television weather reports. (Others just give a summary based on the radar observations at the nearest weather office.) A rotating electronic beam scans the sky within about 150 miles (240 km) from the transmitter. Showers reflect the beam back to the station. That is shown on the screen as a white patch in the right direction and at the right distance, based on the time the echo took to return. When the beam stands still on your screen, as occasionally happens when the television station switches to the weather office circuit, it means the operator there is just measuring the height of the shower or the drop size in the raining cloud.

Long before radar, in 1783 the brothers Montgolfier made a discovery new to the Western world. When you filled a paper bag— their father was in the paper products business—with hot air, it rose to the ceiling. After some experimenting, in the same year they made the first manned hot-air balloon ascent, in Paris.

Still in the same year Jacques Charles filled a balloon with a gas that had recently become available: hydrogen. Hydrogen has much more lifting power than heated air. Unfortunately it also leaks through pores in the balloon. Worse, it is explosively flammable, as the *Hindenburg* tragically demonstrated. Since that disaster helium, heavier than hydrogen but safe, has been used in gas-filled balloons and blimps.

In 1804 Joseph Gay-Lussac made two ascents, sponsored by the French Academy, to measure the magnetism of earth at high elevations. On the first he and another man reached a height of more than 13,000 feet (4 km) and found no change in magnetism. On the second flight Gay-Lussac alone ascended to 23,000 feet (7 km), measured temperature and humidity of the atmosphere, and took air samples at various heights. When he returned to his laboratory, he analyzed the samples and found them all exactly alike. Up to that time one expected the heavier gases to be more abundant near the ground. They would be except for the constant stirring by the winds.

In the United States, in the 1870s and '80s Professor Hazen made some 180 balloon ascents to study temperature and humidity at higher elevations. He even proposed to drift across the Atlantic.

These sporadic flights were great for research but didn't help the forecaster. Not much more than the new weather station atop

Mount Washington in New Hampshire 6,288 feet (1,917 m) above sea level and still in operation.

For daily upper-air data the Weather Bureau went a different route: kites. In 1898 it operated sixteen kite stations, where up to eight kites in tandem were used to take a package of recording instruments aloft. The kites reached routinely 8,000 feet (about 2.5 km), the record height being 23,000 feet (7 km). These heights were measured with theodolites—small telescopes similar to a surveyor's transit—and calculated from the length of line paid out. The "line" was actually piano wire. Hand-powered winches retrieved these miles of wire.

There were difficulties. Winds of at least ten knots were needed to get the whole shebang airborne; rain overloaded the kites; sometimes the wire broke and kite, wire, and instruments were lost. But the program continued, believe it or not, until 1933.

When surface winds were too weak for kite flying, tethered balloons were tried to get the instruments aloft. Then came free-flying balloons, known for some reason as pilot balloons. By tracking them with theodolites from two locations, the direction and speed of the winds aloft could be measured. In 1909 at least eight such balloons were tracked to about 50,000 feet (15 km). A Frenchman had published results of more than five hundred unmanned, instrument-carrying balloon flights five years earlier. His observations reached up to about the same level.

What's magic about that level? As the balloon rises it encounters lowering air pressure. So the gas *inside* the balloon expands and stretches the skin of the bag. At 50,000 feet the atmospheric pressure is only about one-ninth the pressure at sea level. The stretch is too much for the skin. The balloon bursts.

The instrument package carried a note to the finder to return it to the weather bureau. But it was at least hours, more often days before the record of temperature, humidity, etc., reached the weather office. Some showed up months later, many were never turned in.

After 1925 the Weather Bureau, with the cooperation of the Navy and the Army and by contracting with private pilots, obtained upper-air data from daily morning flights of airplanes. At the height of the program planes with meteorographs attached to one wing took off from thirty airfields. At first contract pilots had to reach at least 13,500 feet (about 4 km) to earn their pay. They were paid a 10 per cent bonus for every 1,000 feet (300 m) above that. By 1938 pilots had to reach at least 16,500 feet (about 5 km). Between 1931 and 1938 twelve contract pilots lost their lives, some of them from lack of oxygen trying to earn a bigger bonus.

The next development was the marriage of radio and pilot balloon, the radiosonde. The balloon carried a miniature radio transmitter coupled to the instruments that measure the temperature, humidity, etc. at various levels. One clever solution: Let a barometric switch start the transmission of the data. The first set of data might refer to the level where the atmospheric pressure is 900 mb, the second set to the 850-mb level, the third to the 700-mb level, and so on. The height at the time of transmission can be calculated from the known rate of climb of these balloons.

By tracking the balloon with two theodolites, or better with two radio direction finders, or best by radar, one gets an indication of its drift, hence wind direction and speed aloft.

Even more sophisticated are radio wind sondes that receive signals from Loran or Omega stations on the ground and retransmit them. Loran and Omega were designed to give the navigator of a ship or plane his exact position. Here they tell the operator on the ground where his instrument package is at the moment of transmission.

A totally different type of weather balloon is now in the trial stage: the superpressure constant-level balloon. An ordinary balloon expands on rising in the atmosphere, as we have seen. The new prestretched balloons act as if they had a solid skin. Filled with helium gas and accurately ballasted, they rise to a predetermined level and stay there, just as a submarine can be trimmed to remain at a given depth. One version of this design has been named GHOST (for global horizontal sounding technique). An apt name for a transparent apparition made of two layers of Mylar, each one thousandth of a millimeter (0.00004 inch) thin. Why that thin? One of the design requirements: It must be digestible without harm to the engines of a jet airplane.

Drifting at a constant pressure level—say the important 500-mb level—such balloons could transmit temperature and humidity while giving by their position wind direction and speed since their last report. A few hundred such balloons at several levels would greatly contribute to the details in the daily upper-air maps. Theoretically they would drift at the same level forever. Practically, the gas slowly leaks through the skin, and they start to descend. The weight of raindrops, even dew, pushes them temporarily below their assigned level.

The idea of using rockets for studying the upper atmosphere has been around since 1920. After World War II instrumented rockets made many measurements of the atmosphere and took photographs of large areas of the earth and its cloud cover. They expanded our theoretical knowledge of the uppermost atmosphere. And they whetted the appetite of meteorologists for regular —daily or more frequent—views of the clouds, Nature's own weather map.

How could you get frequent cloud maps? Rockets are out. They are a one-time thing. No Weather Service budget could stand the expense of sending up rockets several times each day from a number of locations. What you want is a television camera permanently in space to send back pictures. The power for the camera and the transmitter is no problem. Photoelectric cells can convert sunlight to electricity.

But how to get the camera up and keep it there? "What goes up must come down," daily experience tells us. That's true of a thrown baseball, a projectile fired from a cannon, and a rocket. They all spend their energy overcoming the gravitational attraction of the earth and slow down. Eventually their speed becomes zero, and they fall back to earth. (Air resistance plays a minor role. Some energy has to be spent to overcome it on the way up; so the highest point of the trajectory will be somewhat lower than it would be without air.)

Let's assume we could give a rocket enough speed so it has just a little of it left when it has climbed to a height—far above the atmosphere—where the attraction of earth is negligible. That rocket would keep going, giving the lie to the what-goes-up statement.

It can be calculated by simple mathematics that we would have to give it a speed of 6.9 miles per second (about 11 km/s). At that speed—the escape velocity—any object would fly off into space. At lesser speeds—but still much greater than those achieved by cannon balls or simple rockets—an object wouldn't quite escape the gravitational field of earth but would forever orbit the earth in an ellipse. Just as the earth's satellite, the moon, does; or as the planets—including earth—do around the sun.

If you wanted to launch such an artificial satellite to carry a television camera for transmitting cloud pictures, you'd better get it high enough to make air resistance negligible. Otherwise it would soon spiral back to earth. Say you settle on an average height of 180 miles (about 290 km). Such a satellite would orbit the earth in ninety minutes, sixteen times a day.

But how to get the necessary speed to put it into that orbit, 4.8 miles per second (7.7 km/s)? Everybody now knows the answer: Use a multistage launch vehicle. The first set of rocket motors lifts the whole clumsy assembly off the ground and gets it up to a certain speed. When the first stage has used up its fuel, it is dropped. The rockets in the second stage are ignited and increase the speed of the now much lighter vehicle. Drop the second stage and repeat the process as necessary.

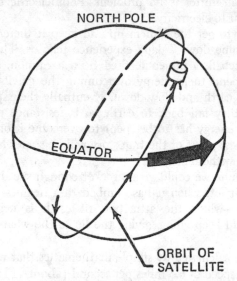

NORTH POLE

EQUATOR

ORBIT OF
SATELLITE

34. Satellite in oblique orbit, at angle
to the equator. Arrow indicates earth
turning under orbiting satellite.

What orbit will you try to achieve? You have several choices. You could launch at an angle to the equator. Then as the earth turns under the inclined orbit—one sixteenth of a full turn between passes of the satellite—the camera would sweep over most of both hemispheres. Only the polar caps would be left out.

You could remedy that lack of coverage by launching a second weather satellite on a polar orbit.

If you are aiming to picture only part of the world, say the Americas, you could launch into a "stationary" orbit. Stationary and orbit sound contradictory. But if you achieve a circular orbit, eastbound over the equator, about 22,000 miles (35,000 km) high, the satellite will travel at the same speed as the point on earth directly below it, once around in about twenty-four hours. For an observer at that point the satellite will always be directly overhead, seemingly stationary. If you miss by a little and the satellite begins to wander off, you can correct its orbit with on-board engines under control from the ground. You can even move the satellite from the middle of the Pacific Ocean to the mouth of the Amazon River and have it stay there until further orders.

Receiving pictures from a satellite in stationary orbit is no problem. The satellite will always be "in sight." For the other two orbits—inclined, and polar—you had better install a videotape system. Then you can ask the satellite for a replay of the tape when it comes within reach of your receiver.

On whatever orbit, with an ordinary television camera you'd lose one half of all picture possibilities. Half the time the satellite spends over areas blacked out by night. Remedy: an infrared system that distinguishes between relatively warm ocean and colder land and clouds. It will also distinguish between snow on the ground and sheets of clouds. They look the same in an ordinary photograph; but the snow is warmer than the cloud tops and so sends more infrared radiation to the camera. Since lower cloud tops are warmer than higher ones, the infrared camera also lets you measure the *height* of clouds.

You know that all that has been done. *Sputnik* in October 1957 and *Explorer 1* a few months later proved that payloads could be put in orbit. *Vanguard 2*, in 1959, sent the first cloud pictures back to earth. Early Tiros weather satellites used orbits inclined to the equator. *Tiros 10* and the ESSA satellites were put in polar orbits. The ATS satellites are kept stationary for many months, then moved at will. *Nimbus* was the first satellite to test infrared cloud photography from space.

It's all routine now. That's how with your evening news you get satellite maps on television with the outlines of the continent, and perhaps cold and warm fronts, added. Besides the still shot, you may also see the "loop," a short movie film each frame of which is a still shot. As time-lapse photography shows the opening of a blossom, so the loop lets you see the development and movement of clouds.

You'll see the cloud masses that trace the fronts, even the whorls around the eye of a hurricane. You'll see the parts of the country where the sky is clear, usually under a high-pressure area,

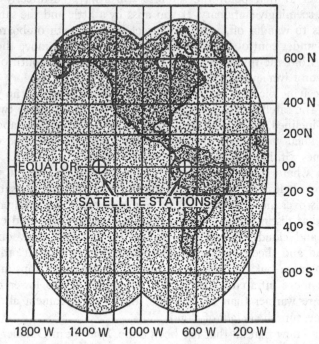

35. Useful coverage by two stationary satellites includes most of the Americas and the oceans from Hawaii to Africa.

and where it is covered by clouds. You can even distinguish between solid cloud cover, flecks of cumulus clouds, and the tracery of cirrus clouds.

All that, up to date, and right in your living room.

16

Forecasting the
Wind: Technique

Everywhere the first method of forecasting the weather—and the wind—was based on local signs. Aristotle and Theophrastus may have *written* about these topics, but the forecasters were the people to whom weather was vitally important: farmers and shipmasters.

When their forecasts were good, they prospered, their peers listened to them, and perhaps they had sons to whom they passed their knowledge of weather signs. Nobody—not even his sons—listened to the farmer who year after year sowed before a drought, started cutting the grain just as the rains came. The shipmaster who missed the signs of an approaching storm might never again be heard from. Perhaps he hadn't lived long enough to have sons. That's the Darwin-Kals theory of the origin of reliable weather signs. Reliable at least locally.

The barometer (and other weather instruments) at first just added another set of local forecasting signs to the observation of wind, clouds, sunsets. . . .

It was the telegraph that made it possible to forecast the weather for large areas. (That's why weather services all over the world started around the same time, in the 1850s.) The telegraph's offspring—transoceanic cables, wireless telegraphy, teleprinters, facsimile picture transmission, radar, and television—helped later.

Once you had a network of telegraph lines, you could have observers report the weather at their location, at set times, to a central office, say in Washington. As soon as their messages started to arrive you could plot their observations in a map that gave an overview, a synopsis, of the conditions all over the country at the time of observation. The synoptic map was such an important step in the process of forecasting the weather that the technique used for the next hundred years could be called *synoptic forecasting.*

A shorthand was soon established for transmitting and plotting the data. A small circle was printed on the map blank for each reporting station, and next to it an identifying number. The message begins with that number. You find the station on the map, then read the next "word," actually a number. A 5 indicates the sky there is five-tenths covered by clouds; you black in one half of the station circle. The next two numerals give the wind direction; you draw an arrow ending at the circle—e.g., straight down for a north wind. Wind speed comes next; you add the proper number of feathers and half-feathers to the arrow. Then you write numerals—always in the same position in relation to the station circle—to indicate numerical data (such as temperature, barometric pressure, amount of rainfall . . .) and draw standard symbols for cloud forms, barometric tendency, weather (e.g., fog, drizzle, rain, snow, thunderstorm). . . . The whole process takes less time than reading about it suggests, and several people can work on different parts of the map.

You now have the raw observations all on one map. The next steps are designed to make it easier to take in the overall weather picture. You draw lines connecting points that reported the same atmospheric pressure, the isobars. If the pressure increases toward the center of an area, you label it H for High; if it decreases, L for Low. You shade areas that reported precipitation. Perhaps on a piece of tracing paper laid over the map you draw lines connecting equal temperatures—say the freezing line, then every round 10 degrees: 40°, 50°, 60° . . . F.

That has been the basic technique for plotting synoptic maps from the beginning. Fronts and air masses were added later. (In the United States in the 1930s.) So now you drew them in different colors (or with their spikes and half-circles) to indicate cold, warm, stationary or occluded—i.e. pinched off from the surface—fronts. And you added the letters identifying air masses from indications of moisture content and temperature.

Plotting the basic data is a mechanical job, requiring mainly accuracy and speed. Drawing the isobars requires more finesse. Few stations report exactly 996, 1,000, 1,004, . . . millibar pressure. So you have to fit the lines between stations. Often it is not obvious where a line goes next. Then you must use our old friend Buys Ballot's law to draw the line from the reported wind direction. In areas covered by few reports, say over the ocean, you may have to fudge the distance to the next isobar from the relation of a reported wind speed to the spacing between isobars. And you must draw all isobars as smooth curves. They must kink, however, at lines of wind shifts and sudden temperature changes—that is, at fronts.

There's more: You must recognize data goofed up by the observer, the telegraph, or the plotter. And you must keep in mind the mountains and valleys that deflect the winds and generally complicate the picture.

But, given a completed synoptic surface map, how would you go about predicting the weather for the next few hours, or perhaps for tomorrow?

The earliest technique was little more than an application of the observation that weather tends to move in an east-northeasterly direction. You'd come up with a slightly better forecast by assuming the weather will move in the direction and at the speed it has in the last twenty-four hours.

Studying past storms, you may find that in certain months storms, say over the United States, move along favorite tracks. Why? And why don't they do so always?

A statistical study of these questions will lead you to new insights. A High here will make a Low there swing far south of the track, for example. Even without knowing the reasons for such aberrant tracks, you'll be tempted to think, "If conditions are such and such, this and that will happen." If you can quickly lay your hands on an earlier synoptic map similar to today's, you can predict tomorrow's weather from the map of the day following the earlier map. This system, *analog forecasting*, doesn't solve the problem either. There are so many variables that the conditions, say over the United States, are never quite the same, however far back you search for a similar pattern.

The introduction of the concepts of air masses, fronts, and wave cyclones (discussed in Chapter 11) into routine forecasts greatly improved their accuracy.

But in all forecasts there is another problem. You, the reader, don't want to know the location and central pressure of a Low tomorrow. You want to know: From what direction will the wind blow tomorrow morning on the lake? How strong? Will we have a wind shift in the middle of the race? Or, will it rain on the golf course in the afternoon?

A central weather office is ideal for receiving and plotting all the data. It can be staffed with the most skilled forecasters. But can it even come close to answering such questions for an area as large as the United States? And as varied as the Mountain states, subtropical southern Florida, Alaska, and the near-desert areas of the Southwest?

So from the beginning of the Weather Service some other organization proved necessary. The large pattern was worked out in Washington, and transmitted to district and local offices. There, other highly trained people, guided by local experience, forecast for much smaller areas by adapting the large developments to the local topography.

Their forecasts for winds—in both direction and speed—were usually good. So were their predictions of temperature. Precipitation—occurrence and amount—was often far off.

Forecasting errors—and the occasional major goofs that upset even temperature and wind forecasts—were not the result of lack of expertise in the central or local office. You already know what caused them: conditions in the *upper* air.

To put it differently: A two-dimensional synoptic map is not enough to forecast the weather. To forecast the surface movement of Highs and Lows, their strengthening and weakening, and the probability of precipitation, you need upper-air soundings. You must know pressure, temperature, humidity, wind direction and speed, at upper levels, right into the stratosphere.

Take just one modern forecasting rule: Surface Lows move in the direction of the upper-air flow; their forward speed is typically 30 per cent of the wind speed at the 500-mb level (about 18,000 feet or 5,500 m). You can see how that one rule would give you a better forecast than yesterday's movement, storm tracks, and average speeds for the month, or similar maps from other years.

Upper-air maps were drawn already from kite observations and used with rules like the one just mentioned for improved forecasts. Upper-air maps look much simpler than surface maps. There are fewer Highs and Lows. Mountains create fewer problems. The winds, as you'll recall, blow virtually parallel to the lines that indicate barometric pressure, the height contours. (Compare figures 16 and 17.)

Even from observations that give only pressure heights you can draw the wind direction; from the spacing between contours you get the wind speed at that level. (With just a little trouble you can correct wind data for temperature influences.) And twice a day, at noon and midnight Greenwich time, you get radio wind data for seven or more levels from many stations, several dozen over the contiguous United States alone.

Drawing these maps isn't difficult. But what human forecaster can keep a surface map and seven upper-air maps in his mind at the same time? And the interaction between upper atmosphere and surface weather isn't as simple as the rule I've used as an example.

Enters the computer. You feed it the same data humans used to draw the synoptic surface map, and it draws it for you, shading and all. You give it the upper-air data, and it plots contours, temperatures, and humidities at every level. And it remembers all the millions of individual data that go into just one set of maps. If you have given it the proper instructions—equations—it prints maps of the conditions at the surface and at any desired level in the upper air, for six, twelve, twenty-four, . . . hours from now. That's *numerical* weather prediction, or *dynamic* weather forecasting, the method now in use.

The computer is programmed to filter out observations disturbed by purely local influences. And like a human plotter, it will discard observations that are likely to be mistakes.

That brings up a story too good to leave out, although I have been unable to find an eyewitness. John von Neumann and his group had programmed the first computer to plot the maps and project them into the future. To test the program, they fed the computer old weather data and compared the computed maps with the actual conditions on the next day. The results were quite respectable.

Then one forecaster in the room suggested they use the data of the biggest goof in his career. He had forecast routine weather for New York City, and 28 inches (more than 70 cm) of snow fell.

The computer went through its routine and came up with a perfectly routine prognostic map. Then the forecaster remembered that on that day he had discarded two garbled reports. One from a station in Nova Scotia, the other a ship's report. So had the computer

They re-entered the two thrown-out observations, and canceled the "disregard unlikely data" instruction. Out came a map that clearly foretold a violent clash of air masses over New York City the next day.

Computers have become more sophisticated and their programming is constantly being improved. Today, for instance, they'll print you a map of the whole country showing the probability of rainfall in the next twelve to sixty hours everywhere. Or the minimum and maximum surface temperature.

These maps are transmitted by wire to regional and local forecast offices. Modified by these centers, they end up in your local newspaper, and weather reports on radio and television. They also decide whether your local department store in Thursday's advertising will feature air-conditioners or rainwear.

A chart of the Atlantic showing wave heights is sent by radio facsimile to ships at sea. It lets a tanker captain pick the most economical—not necessarily the shortest—route.

Other maps produced by computer make commercial aviation the routine operation it has become day and night, summer and winter.

Where does all this technological progress leave *you*?

If the weather, and especially the wind, is important to you, and you have lived in the same area for some time, you have probably some weather signs that work for you. Perhaps you have a barometer and get indications from its level. Perhaps it's an aneroid and you watch the needle jump, up or down.

Some people use a table, which comes with some barometers,

and is supposed to predict the weather for the next twenty-four hours from the level of the barometer, its tendency, and the present wind direction. Others use a more sophisticated-looking gadget that also takes present sky conditions into account.

But few of us would seriously argue that any of these signs and rules are consistently better than the forecasts made by experts with access to data from all over the country—and the world—and not just taken on the ground but in the upper atmosphere. Or that the clouds you see predict the weather better than those seen by a satellite and interpreted by experts.

Of course, some forecasts of the weather people are wide of the mark. Some of these errors have a simple explanation: The weather office must make a single forecast. The public wouldn't put up with a forecast that read, "If the High remains stationary, the weekend will be sunny and mild. On the other hand, if it begins to move out, prepare for two days of drizzle, followed by rain or snow."

I remember the forecast for a long Easter weekend in Vancouver, Canada, a difficult place for a forecaster. Few upweather reports and 4,000-foot (1,200-m) mountains right behind the city. On the Thursday evening news the weatherman read the official forecast: Dismal. The weatherman happened to be a personal friend of mine. So I knew he was a sailor—he had sailed to Tahiti and back—an aircraft pilot, and a sailplane enthusiast. A weatherwise fellow, who had just come from the situation room at the weather office. After the official forecast he added, "This forecast is based on the assumption that the clouds now massed offshore will continue to drift eastward, hang up on our mountains, and unload their Pacific moisture. But if the lowest clouds rise only another one thousand feet, they will clear the mountains, and we'll have a beautiful weekend." I went sailing Friday and Saturday, skiing Sunday and Monday. Beautiful.

Usually you can't do better than to get the official forecast from your newspaper, radio, or television set. It's fun to visualize the winds all over the map, or the satellite photograph, and to understand why the forecast calls for a wind shift tomorrow afternoon. And from today's temperatures and the front near you, you can almost predict temperatures to come: Your temperature will be replaced by the temperatures now reported *behind* the front.

You may enjoy these little games. But when the weather bureau predicts severe thunderstorms for your area—with their potential for tornadoes—or broadcasts hurricane warnings, you had better listen. And you'll be wise not to ignore small-craft and travelers' warnings either.

About the only thing you can do better than the experts is forecasting a short time in advance for a very small area. The weather service is not likely to tell you that it'll rain hard in five minutes over the tennis courts; the black cloud in the west does.

Often you can adapt the area forecast to your small patch of the world. Say you live in a narrow valley that runs north-south. You may have noticed that at your house it hardly ever blows from the west. A forecast northwest wind is likely to become a north wind where you are.

Or perhaps you live on the west slope of a mountain. Even when there is only a small probability of showers in the forecast, experience will make you expect rain in summer, snow in winter, whenever low clouds approach from the west.

And sometimes you may notice a minor goof of the weather people early enough to take advantage of it. Say the forecast for your area—several counties—predicted rain for the afternoon. At noon the sky is still clear at your place except for some high cirrus clouds. How about arranging a golf game for three o'clock? (The front has probably traveled a little slower than expected.)

On another day there is no mention of showers in the morning forecast. But you see some rather dark clouds upwind in the sky when you take in the paper. Should you water the shrubs before going to work? I'd save the work and the water. If it doesn't rain, I can water in the evening.

Are the official forecasts likely to get better? For the next twelve to twenty-four hours they are already pretty good. In fact they are a lot better than most people realize. The Weather Service constantly monitors its own performance and reports that about 85 per cent of forecasts come true.

It's a difficult matter to measure. Say you forecast a high temperature of 70–75° F for a city. It may be 75° downtown, 70° at the airport; 100 per cent accurate. But what if it is 76° downtown, 69° at the airport? Would you consider that off? If you let that pass, how about 77° and 68°?

Temperature forecasts are easily verified. But how about other forecasts—rain, for instance. You predict 50 per cent probability of showers for the state as a whole. It rains in some parts of the state, but not a drop falls on the parched lawns of many other citizens. They are likely to call your forecast a miss.

Some little improvement in short-range forecasts can be expected. Work goes forward on several fronts. More observations, from GHOST balloons and ocean weather buoys for example. Better programs for the computer. As now set up, the computer cannot yet digest all the temperature data satellites supply.

The hope is that someday the forty-eight-hour forecast will be verified as well as the twenty-four-hour forecasts are now.

Long-range forecasts, more than five days into the future, are a different matter. People who are working in that field hold out little hope for much better forecasts. And even for that short time the forecasts will not tell you whether you should wear a cotton dress, a sweater, or a raincoat at a given day and place. These forecasts, the experts think, will always be in generalities: areas where temperature or precipitation will be normal, or higher or lower than normal.

Two weeks ahead is about as long as anyone hopes to give meaningful forecasts. There is little hope in such forecasts for prediction of wind direction and speed, except for a general hemispherical flow pattern. No hope for predicting hurricanes that far in advance. And—if that were logically possible—even less hope for tornado warnings.

17

Power from the Wind

For many centuries the winds moved people and freight along shores and across oceans. Some wind-powered freighters survived well into this century, carrying low-cost cargo: grain from Australia, salt from the West Indies and lumber on the return trip. Today, with some local exceptions and a few training ships, the wind fills only the sails of craft used for pleasure. Racing, cruising, or just messing around.

The wind seems too good to serve only sailors, kites, and wind chimes. Why don't we use it as a source of power?

It has been grinding grain since the seventh century. (We still call wind engines, even when they drive pumps or generate electricity, wind*mills.*) The earliest known windmill, in Persia, was a simple affair: The sails—we still call them sails, whatever their shape and material—mounted around a vertical shaft, drove one of the millstones. Oddly, the sails were mounted *inside* the building, and *below* the stone. The vertical shaft has one great advantage. It doesn't matter from what direction the wind blows. That's why we still use it in the cup anemometer.

In the twelfth century windmills were built in Europe, their design perhaps brought back by the crusaders. These windmills were advanced models with sails in the vertical plane on a horizontal shaft. Like a child's whirligig.

Having a horizontal shaft drive the millstone was no problem. Already the ancient Romans had developed the needed gearing for their water-driven mills. But the sails had to face the wind. Solution: Turn the whole building by muscle power, aided by winches. In a later invention you only had to turn the top of the building, which carried the sail. Much later mills were made self-tending: A fantail like a weather vane turns the sail into the wind.

In the fifteenth century windmills were used extensively in Holland to drain land. In the first design a scoop wheel, resembling the wheel of a water-driven mill, was mounted directly on the main shaft. If you had supplied flowing water to the scoops, you would have had a water-powered wind-making machine.

Similar devices had been used for irrigation in China for centuries. They are said to have been built first by millwrights brought from Persia—with or without their consent—by Genghis Khan.

In the nineteenth century steam power competed with wind power. But that was also the period of the greatest improvements in windmills. Sails were made adjustable; furled as in a roller blind, or "feathered" as in a Venetian blind. And finally metal vanes arranged like the spokes of a wheel were mass produced.

In 1902 you could order a pumping windmill from Sears, Roebuck and Company with 8-foot steel wheel for $15.05 painted, $16.65 galvanized. (Tower extra; fully guaranteed.) With an 8- to 12-foot (2.4- to 3.7-m) wheel on a 60-foot (18-m) tower, that windmill would lift 300 to 900 gallons (1,000 to 3,400 l) per hour 100 feet (30 m).

At high wind speeds a simple mechanism automatically reduced the surface presented to the wind. At one time an estimated six million similar windmills were working in the United States. All the maintenance needed was some grease—later models were self-oiling—and some paint to keep the rust down.

For pumping water you could hardly design a cheaper, simpler device. You could also make the same basic windmill drive a generator to produce electricity. But gasoline and diesel engines won out over wind-powered machines. It seemed easier to put a barrel of fuel on the pickup and drive to your little power plant. Then—under FDR—a network of wires began to distribute cheap, reliable, noiseless electricity from central generators to every corner of the United States. Now all you have to do is mail a check once a month.

But a quarter of a million windmills are still standing in the rural United States. And windmill repairmen are again available.

Wind costs nothing and is much more generously distributed

over the land than usable water power. As fuel prices—and with them rates for electricity—rise, can we turn back to the wind for power?

Let's first look at power for a single household or a cluster of buildings.

In most places there are periods of total calm. For efficient power generation a gentle breeze, say of 3 knots, is not much better than a calm. But for several hours a day, especially on a hilltop, you may get enough wind flow to supply all the electricity you need. Unfortunately you can't store the wind for the time when you want it. But that problem can be solved.

If you live in a skyscraper in New York City, or a high-rise condominium in Florida, you probably wouldn't consider rolling your own electricity. But a friend of mine, cruising on a sailboat in the Bahamas, built his own wind generator. On the forward side of the mainmast he mounted a propeller, salvaged from a light aircraft, and let a V belt drive a generator off a junked truck. Whenever he was at anchor, his craft would lie into the wind; he'd release the lashing that kept the propeller parallel to the mast when he sailed and charge his batteries. The batteries ran his lights, radio, stereo, and bilge pump.

Batteries are essential in most installations. The wind may not blow, or may blow too weakly during periods of greatest demand. As every car owner has found out, lead batteries only last a few years. But batteries with a life of ten years or more have been around since 1900, when Edison invented them.

In hill country storage batteries can be replaced by water storage. Here's one method. A mail-order-type wind pump, or several such pumps, lift water to a storage pond. Perhaps a natural pond, or a small hollow that only needs bulldozing a short earth dam to make it into a lake. The water from the storage pond drives a turbine to generate electricity when you want it. The process can be made completely automatic. The wind, whenever it blows, drives the pump. The first switch turned on starts the downhill flow of water; the last switch turned off stops it. The water collects in a lower pond near the windmill and is used over and over.

In flat country, in Maryland, an artist built a wind generator mounted on a 50-foot (15-m) tower. It pumps his water, supplies all his lights, even powers a washing machine.

A man in Maine runs television, power tools, vacuum cleaner, and sewing machine by wind-generated electricity. He figures that over twenty years the electricity he uses will cost him about half what it would cost to generate it with a diesel plant. The original installation cost of his wind generator was less than the electric company wanted for bringing the power from the nearest high-voltage line to his house.

Of course, if you already have electricity, you could use the tailor-made kind for standby and peak load. Or for the appliances with the greatest appetite for kilowatts.

If a large company mass-produced and leased or financed a package plant, including batteries, many households could become electrically self-sufficient. Not just in the United States but in rural and suburban areas all around the world.

Grumman Aerospace and Princeton University are reported to be working on such a package. Here are some preliminary figures: Their 25-foot (about 8-m) sail would generate 5 kilowatts when the wind blows at 11 knots. Target price about $4,000 including batteries. In a favorable location such a generator would produce a generous 12,500 kwh a year, which at present rates might cost you $400.

The same 12,500 kwh produced in a large generating plant would use twenty barrels of fuel. If only 10 per cent of the seventy million households in the United States switched to wind power, their average consumption of 7,000 kwh hours per year would save 214,000 barrels of oil—or the equivalent in natural gas—each *day*.

Large installations, as for a power company, are a different matter. Banks of batteries are out of the question. The wind generator feeds directly into the power lines. Other generators supply the current when the wind falters or fails. Even well below the wind speed for which the plant has been designed, it contributes significantly to the total output of a power company.

One such large installation was the Smith-Putnam generator on Grandpa's Knob near Rutland, Vermont. The Central Vermont Public Service Corporation built it in the early 1940s. A two-bladed propeller 175 feet (53 m) in diameter was mounted on a tower 108 feet (33 m) high. The generator, on the same shaft as the propeller, acted as a counterweight. The entire assembly was made to turn into the wind by a small motor controlled by a wind vane. It worked as a routine generating station for sixteen months in all.

But there were troubles not connected with the design. First, one of the main bearings failed. Bad luck; most bearings outlast their engines. When the bearing had been replaced after long war-caused delays, one of the blades failed due to a defective weld. The entire experiment had cost 1.25 million dollars.

Other large generators have been built in France, Denmark, Russia, and Great Britain.

In 1974 the National Aeronautics and Space Administration (NASA), as part of a wind-energy program, started construction of an experimental wind generator in Ohio. In appearance it resembles the unlucky Vermont installation. The two-bladed pro-peller, mounted on a 100-foot (30-m) tower, sweeps a circle 125 feet (38 m) in diameter. Estimated cost around $900,000. De-signed capacity 100 kw; estimated annual production 180,000 kwh. That's not much for a power company. The idea is to operate a whole "farm" of such generators at one suitable location. One imaginative design has them suspended, like traffic lights, on a cable stretched between towers.

Farms of many wind machines are not a new idea. Just before their plane landed at Nassau in the Bahamas many visitors have seen a field of windmills built to pump the city's water.

Actually several small farms, or towers carrying only a few units on one cable, are more productive for a power company. When the wind drops below the cut-in speed at one installation, it may produce energy at another location. Also a single tornado would not jeopardize the entire wind-powered output.

The location of wind plants is most important. Obviously a site with the fewest hours of calms and light winds is best. But winds over land vary greatly in strength. And the power the wind can generate does not depend directly on the speed of the wind but increases with the cube of that speed.

Say one site records an average wind speed of 6 knots for so many hours a year. Another nearby site records 7 knots for the same number of hours. The second site will produce almost 60 per cent more power. If you can find an 8-knot site, you'd increase your power output 137 per cent over the first location.

A new profession has been born: wind prospector. His tools are not geologist's hammer and geiger counter but recording anemometers and temporary towers to mount them.

Engineers are not restricted by the existing land. They can increase the windspeed by cutting and filling and creating artificial mountain passes.

In suitable terrain the storage-pond scheme may work on a large scale. A series of wind-driven pumps would get water to a higher level, perhaps back to an existing lake after it has run through a conventional turbine and produced electricity. That, in effect, is storing the wind for the hours of peak load. Aeolus might be jealous of such a wind-storage system. It's much more efficient than his cave. Water, you'll recall, is about eight hundred times as dense as air and so is that much easier to warehouse.

The search for suitable wind-power sites is not restricted to land areas. The Great Lakes and seacoasts are being intensively studied. Before long you may see wind generators anchored like lightships off the Oregon coast, or topping Texas-tower-like structures on stilts.

Carrying the electricity generated offshore to land is no problem. Suitable cables are in use now. But there are other ways. You could, for instance, use the electricity generated in Lake Michigan to produce hydrogen from the lake water, then pipe the gas ashore, store it, and burn it in a conventional power plant during peak demand hours.

Engineers are also working on better ways to extract power from the wind. One design that merits more study, according to some experts, is the S rotor. You have seen small versions of it in some ventilators. The name derives both from its shape and from the name of its chief investigator, a Finnish engineer, S. J. Savonius.

A patent for perhaps the most elegant recent invention of an aerogenerator was applied for in 1974. The principle is shown in figure 37A. Wind flowing over the curved, perforated surface creates a partial vacuum. Many such bulbs could be attached to a hollow tower. Air allowed to enter near the bottom could drive a vertical wind turbine, which in turn would drive a conventional generator. Instead of many bulbs, one or several disks attached to the tower might prove more efficient in wind-tunnel tests. Such a mushroom, with several caps perhaps, or airfoils shaped like the

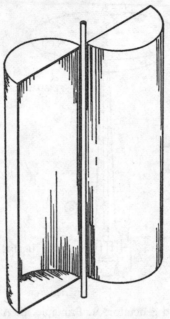

36. S rotor, a self-starting, vertical wind sail

wing of a plane, just might be the wind generator of the future. It would work with the wind from any direction and would have no external moving parts. High wind speeds would be no problem, you'd just shutter the turbine. Gustiness of the wind would be smoothed out by the large volume of air in the tower. And the heavy machinery is where it belongs, near the foundations.

A totally different approach, currently in the backyard-experiment stage, has been suggested. It creates a man-made whirlwind to drive a turbine generator like the one just described. You might call it a chimney without walls. (A conventional chimney of any practical height and cross section doesn't create enough suction.) A ring of heat is produced near the ground. The resulting updraft together with the existing wind produces a vortex, just as an oil fire in California once produced a tornado. If the vortex can be made stable, it just might do the trick.

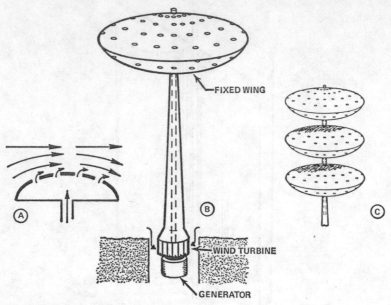

37. Fixed-wing wind generator. A. Principle. B. A single-wing installation. C. A possible three-wing installation.

The environmental effect of wind machines is negligible. Short of blowing down in a hurricane, what harm can they do? (In small installations the tower can be lowered like the mast of a Dutch barge when passing under a bridge.) There's no emission from stacks, no hot-water discharge, no problem with atomic wastes. The only pollution would be visual. I think most of us could put up with some towers in remote areas of the landscape.

The "fuel" is free, abundant, and inexhaustible. Nobody can make it into atomic bombs.

By conservative estimate *usable* wind power equals the present electric-generating capacity of the world. That's from all sources of power: hydroelectric, fossil fueled, and atomic.

Wind will not replace all these other power sources overnight. The technology for atomic power generation has been around for thirty years and is just beginning to be felt on a worldwide scale. But one expert predicts that in the 1990s wind power may provide at least 10 per cent of the United States' power needs, at costs competitive with conventional power sources.

In a recent study for the Energy Research Administration two engineers predict that building and maintaining giant windmills will become a major industry. Within twenty years thousands of windmills placed around the country could save the equivalent of two billion barrels of oil a year. They found that in some areas of the United States wind energy is already cheaper now than fossil-fuel energy. And everyone expects fuel prices to rise as reserves are used up.

If you are interested in a single-family unit, a good place to start looking for names of makers of complete installations and kits would be the October 1976 issue of *Popular Mechanics* at your public library.

18

Winds Link the World

Without winds life on earth would be very different from the life we know. I don't just mean that the discovery of and traffic with the Americas and Australia would have had to wait a few hundred more years until steamships were ready. Nor that on occasion the wind decided the outcome of battles, changing the history of entire nations. These are mere sidelines of the wind.

The wearing away of mountains and the creation of fertile land are also relatively unimportant.

The plants that depend on the wind for pollination could never have developed. (Have the bees and butterflies that pollinate other plants perhaps been distributed over the world by the wind?) The forests that depend on the wind to carry their seeds could never have spread. And all land animals—and ultimately man—depend on plants, consuming plants directly or eating plant-fed animals.

And where could plants and animals live on an earth without wind?

We have seen that the earth as a whole loses as much heat to space as it receives from the sun. But at any one place the outgo and income of radiation is unlikely to balance. In the northern hemisphere there is an annual balance near latitude 38°. In the southern hemisphere the line of balance is not far from that latitude. Between these latitudes more heat arrives, year after year, than dissipates. Without winds the land in that area—more than half of all land—would get warmer all the time. Between these lines and the poles the yearly heat loss exceeds the income. Without winds the land there would get steadily colder.

The winds even out the temperature differences and make most of the land areas fit for the life of plants, animals, and man. Most of that heat transfer is carried out, day by day, by the whorls in the westerlies. And on occasion hurricanes carry spectacular loads of heat away from the tropics.

That's not all the wind does for life. Life on earth needs water. Give an area less than 10 inches (25 cm) of annual rainfall, and you have created a desert. All precipitation is water that has been turned into water vapor on the surface. Yet in any one year most land areas receive more precipitation than they have supplied to the atmosphere.

How can that go on year after year?

One might think the evaporation over the oceans makes up the deficit over land. But it's more complicated than that. A zone from about latitude 35° N to the Arctic, and one from a similar latitude to the Antarctic run in the red even when you take the ocean areas into account. (The arctic and antarctic zones themselves have a slight surplus of precipitation. But precipitation is scant, and the formation of water vapor over ice is low.) The eddies in the westerlies day by day make up the moisture deficit, again helped occasionally by hurricanes.

Near the equator there is a zone, about 25 degrees of latitude wide in each hemisphere, where rainfall also exceeds evaporation even when you consider the oceans. The trade winds in each hemisphere make up that deficit.

All these winds, and the seasonal monsoons, so well distribute the greening moisture over the globe that only a few pockets remain barren—deserts.

There are no apparent surface winds to carry air from one hemisphere to the other, from the northeast trade wind belt to the belt of the southeast trade winds or the other way around. But there *is* an interchange. That was first dramatically demonstrated by the eruption of Krakatoa in 1883. That volcano in the Sunda Strait, between Java and Sumatra, sent up a black cloud 90,000 feet (27 km) high, dropping ashes and pumice over a circle 50 miles (80 km) wide. Thick enough to hamper ship traffic through the strait. On nearby islands the people had to burn their lights during daylight hours for three days. Finally Krakatoa blew up—or, perhaps more accurately, fell in on itself—with a bang heard 3,000 miles (4,800 km) away.

The ashes thrown up into what we now would call the strato-sphere traveled around the world. Spreading out, they provided for the next year spectacular, gory sunsets from Scandinavia to Capetown.

But the world seems to have forgotten the lesson. For several years nuclear devices were tested in out-of-the-way places in the Pacific and in Siberia. Then in a plant at Rochester, New York, film fogged. The trouble was traced to the gelatine used in its manufacture. It had been made from hides and hooves of cattle that in Argentina had eaten grass contaminated by radioactive fallout. At another time milk in the American Midwest turned ra-dioactive. Finally the major nuclear powers agreed not to test in the atmosphere any more. But traces of radioactivity from earlier tests, and from later tests by countries not concerned with the test ban, can be found in the snow and ice of the Antarctic and the Arctic.

Both in Krakatoa's eruption and in nuclear tests, what was put into the atmosphere were particles. (Television weathermen call them *particulates*; it sounds more learned.) Small bits of matter.

They have to be small to be supported by the wind. Large parti-cles, like garbage-can lids and beach umbrellas, fall out rapidly under the influence of gravity.

In the lower atmosphere small particles will come back to earth within a matter of days or, at most, weeks. They bump into other particles—including the ever-present salt particles from sea spray—stick together, and become too heavy to stay airborne. They also may attract minute water droplets, which, joining with others, form drops that finally fall as rain.

Atmospheric scientists are prone to talk about *aerosols*. The definition: a suspension of fine solid or liquid particles in a gas. You know them as smoke, fog, and mists (natural, or from an in-secticide fogger or aerosol can).

By whatever name—particles, particulates, or aerosols—they quite literally gravitate back to earth and so are concentrated in the lowest 10,000 feet (3 km) of the atmosphere before being washed out by rain.

It does not rain in the stratosphere. Particles from Krakatoa, a nuclear explosion in the atmosphere, or whatever source, once above the troposphere will stay there a long time. A matter of years. But you'll recall from the chapter on jet streams that the boundary between troposphere and stratosphere is not like the skin of a balloon. I compared it to the overlapping plates of a suit of armor. So eventually the aerosols will find their way through the chinks—where the jet streams blow—back to the troposphere. And to the ground.

We are sending staggering quantities of particles into the atmosphere. In smoke for instance. One estimate gives twenty million tons a year for the United States alone. (Here and in the following figures it doesn't matter whether you read that as short tons of 2,000 pounds, long tons, or metric tons; the difference between these units—at most 10 per cent—is less than the likely error of the estimate.)

Photographs from orbiting satellites show three persistent plumes of concentrated particles over the world. One such dust cloud spreads downwind from North America over the Atlantic. The second trails from Asia and Japan over the Pacific. Both of these can be traced to industrialized areas. The third plume, over the Indian Ocean, is believed to be wind-borne sand.

The mixture of water vapor and smoke particles, perhaps with a few other goodies thrown in, becomes visible as pea-soup fog. That kind of fog is called London-type fog. Its origin and composition is quite different from the smog over, say, Los Angeles, about which you'll read later in this chapter.

Besides particles, man sends fabulous amounts of *gases* into the atmosphere.

Carbon dioxide alone accounts for fifteen billion tons a year. It is a normal end product of the burning of peat, wood, coal, fuel oil, gasoline, and natural gas. But it's hard to believe that every man, woman, and child in the world should dispose of almost four tons of that gas per year.

But even that quantity is only about one fifth of the annual turnover of carbon dioxide in nature. Growing plants borrow it from the air; when they decompose, they pay it back. Leaves and annuals have the loan for only a few months; shrubs for a few years; the trunks, roots, and branches of trees for at most a few centuries. The fossil fuels we burn—coal, petroleum products, and natural gas—have had the carbon locked up for some millions of years.

As a good gas should, carbon dioxide distributes itself all over the world, and from the bottom of the atmosphere to the top of the stratosphere. At present the worldwide concentration is about 330 parts per million parts of air (ppm). Our burning of fossil fuels should add about 2 ppm a year to the carbon dioxide content of the air. The measured increase is less than half that. Where does the rest go? Probably it is absorbed by the oceans, which already hold some sixty times as much carbon dioxide as the air.

As far as anybody knows, the slight annual increase in sea and air is harmless to life in all its forms. And since air is more than one fifth oxygen, we won't miss the amount of that gas tied up in carbon dioxide.

Carbon monoxide is a different matter. Every year the world throws 200–300 million tons of it in the atmosphere, one third of that over the United States. It is the product of poor combustion as in a kerosene heater in a closed room. But more than 90 per cent of the total discharge comes from the exhaust of cold, idling, or misadjusted automobile engines.

Inhaled, carbon monoxide combines with some of the hemoglobin in your blood. That reduces the blood's capacity to carry oxygen, resulting in a diminished oxygen supply to the brain. So impaired mental function is the first symptom.

Concentration levels of 50 ppm are common on city streets. Two hours of inhaling that mixture will cause observable impairment. Several hundred parts of carbon monoxide per million parts of air have been measured in traffic tunnels and underground garages. At only 200 ppm impairment becomes noticeable after a mere fifteen minutes.

Where carbon monoxide gets a chance to spread freely, the concentration drops rapidly to the average worldwide value in the troposphere (0.1–0.2 ppm). That concentration diminishes rapidly as you get into the stratosphere. Perhaps it combines there with oxygen to form harmless carbon dioxide.

Oddly, repeated measurements have failed to detect any annual increase in carbon monoxide concentration in the atmosphere. That's especially odd since the present total concentration is equivalent to only a few years of carbon monoxide emission. So little of it is found in sea water that it is unlikely that it ends up in the oceans.

The world throws some 150 million tons of *sulfur dioxide* into the atmosphere, 20 per cent of that over the United States. Main sources: industry and electric power plants.

Sulfur is plentiful in sea water. There it ranks just after magnesium, which in turn comes right after the elements that make up common salt. But salt in sea water is some thirty times more abundant than sulfur. Some of that sulfur gets into the atmosphere as sea spray. More sulfur is released by volcanoes and some hot springs. All living matter absorbs small quantities of sulfur and returns it when it decomposes (some of it with the smell of rotten eggs). Ultimately rain returns all that sulfur to the oceans.

The natural turnover of sulfur in the atmosphere in a year is only about twice the quantity released by man.

One effect of sulfur constantly added to the atmosphere by man is this: The rains are getting more acid. (You can taste the acid in a pea-soup fog when sulfur from soft coal produces sulfuric acid on your tongue.) When we first began to measure the acidity of rain, it was no more acid than a potato. Now rains are often as acid as a tomato. Near industrial areas they have sometimes been measured as acid as lemon juice.

That's serious. In lemon-juice concentrations acid rain kills plants and freshwater fish. But long before that level of acidity is reached, such rain stunts the growth of plants of many kinds. Reports of diminished yields due to chronic acid rain include such diverse cash crops as grains, soybeans, oranges, and pine trees.

Oddly, part of the increase in acidity of the rain may have been caused by our efforts to rid industrial smoke of solid particles. Some of the particles now scrubbed out were capable of neutralizing the acids formed from sulfur dioxide (and oxides of nitrogen).

In the words of the Cornell University scientists who reported this state of affairs, "We have transformed local soot problems into regional acid rain problems." The answer of course, is not to scrub the scrubbers but to find economically feasible ways to remove or neutralize the acid-forming gases.

Oxides of nitrogen are released into the atmosphere at an annual rate of about fifty million tons worldwide, twenty million tons over the United States alone. More than half of that comes from the exhausts of automobiles (gasoline), trucks (diesel fuel), and jet planes (kerosene).

Nitrogen and oxygen—in that order—are the two most plentiful gases in the atmosphere. So where is the harm in adding a combination of these two gases, which already make up 99 per cent of all air. Simply this: Oxides of nitrogen, even in small quantities, when the sun shines on them create photochemical smog, Los Angeles-type fog. Unburned hydrocarbons from the same exhausts enter into the brew and create some more unpleasantness.

But why Los Angeles? Sunshine and exhausts are plentiful there. But there's more. If the oxides of nitrogen and other gases were distributed upward by rising air currents, and distributed by the wind, they would soon be diluted to insignificant concentrations. But over Los Angeles a temperature inversion—higher air temperature than at a level just below it—much of the time limits the vertical dilution. And the mountains that hem in the Los Angeles Basin on the downwind side hinder the sideways spread of the air trapped under the inversion.

Such inversions, coupled with light winds, are found throughout most of the year on all subtropical west coasts. No worse places could have been found for such cities as Casablanca, Capetown, and Santiago, Chile.

Inversions often also appear inland, and over other than subtropical areas. Here is one common mechanism: During the night the ground has cooled, and with it the lowest few hundred feet (or meters) of air. That makes the morning air below cooler than the air above it. Gases warmed near the ground can rise only to the warm level. The inversion keeps a lid on the air below. Vertical mixing is restricted to the layer below the inversion. The winds are frequently light in the morning, limiting rapid horizontal spreading. Now fire up a few factory chimneys, put a few more coal-fired electric generators on line, start the go-to-work traffic, and add sunshine. You have just manufactured Los Angeles smog.

Donora in the Monongahela valley, southeast of Pittsburgh, is far from the subtropics and the West Coast. In October 1948 an inversion lingered for three days under a stalled high-pressure area. Local plants discharged their usual load of gases into the calm air. On the third day one half of the fourteen thousand people in town were ill; twenty died.

In this and similar disasters we see a failure of the wind to do one of its expected jobs. Much as we don't give a thought to where our trash goes until a strike of sanitation workers makes the stuff pile up under our noses, figuratively and literally.

There is another concern: Will all the stuff—particles and gases —we throw into the atmosphere change our climate? Locally? Over large regions?

The climate of an area, or even the world, is sensitive to small changes in temperature. A city raises the temperature of the downwind countryside by 2–4 degrees Fahrenheit (1–2 degrees Celsius) and increases the rainfall there. And it takes only a worldwide drop in temperature of the same order to create an ice sheet over most of the world. A similar rise in temperature would gradually melt the ice in the Arctic and Antarctic and would raise the sea level to reach the twenty-fifth floor of a building in New York or any other coastal city.

We know there have been several ice ages, the last one ending less than ten thousand years ago. None of the several theories that account for these frigid periods is universally accepted.

Will particles thrown into the atmosphere bring on another period of cooler climate? The question has no simple answer. You would expect the particles in the atmosphere to keep some sunlight from reaching the ground. That should lower the temperature at the surface. Actually most of the particles we have been considering absorb sunlight and help to *warm* the air in the lower atmosphere.

In 1963 Mount Agung on Bali (not far from Krakatoa) put vast quantities of ashes into the stratosphere. Measured result: A warming of around 5 degrees Fahrenheit (2–3 degrees Celsius) in the upper atmosphere between latitudes 40° S and 20° N. It took eight years before the temperature there returned to the values recorded before the Agung eruption.

Whether additional particles in the lower atmosphere will cause warming or cooling depends on several factors: their size, chemical composition, and color.

The question you may ask now is this: Is the world still warming, recovering as it were from the last cold episode? Or is it already chilling in the beginning of the next one?

The question is not new. In a study published in 1868 Elias Loomis examined temperature observations for one century in the United States and Europe. His conclusion: no significant change in mean temperature.

We now have data for another hundred years and from many more places. But the question is still open. It is similar to the one you may have asked at the seashore: "Are the waves now a bit higher than they were a little earlier, or is the tide rising?" Or in another field: "Are today's stock market quotations a sign of a collapsing bull market, or a mere technical adjustment?" On another day: "Do the prices reflect a continuing upward trend, or are they due to covering of short sales?"

Statisticians are supposed to be able to calculate trends. (Then why don't they all become rich in the stock market?) But in climatology the data are confusing. Example: In Greenland glaciers are receding as if the warm-up were still going on; in Antarctica snow is accumulating indicating just the opposite.

Great interest centers on carbon dioxide levels in the atmosphere. You'll remember that this gas is involved in what has been called the "greenhouse effect" (Chapter 9). The man-made net increase of carbon dioxide in the atmosphere—measured as one part per million parts of air per year—could easily raise the temperature in the lower atmosphere. That sounds like a logical argument.

And that's not all. We have seen that the oceans are an enormous storehouse of carbon dioxide. Now it is a known fact that the warmer the water the less carbon dioxide it can hold. (You have watched soda water go "flat" as it gets warm.) That process would release more carbon dioxide into the atmosphere as the ocean surface warmed. You have the makings of a chain reaction.

Taking all the known laws into account, a group of scientists at the Massachusetts Institute of Technology programmed a computer to calculate the results of a dramatic threefold increase of the carbon dioxide content of the atmosphere. That's 1,000 ppm, against the present level of about 330 ppm. Result: Virtually no warming in the troposphere; some *cooling* in the stratosphere.

Do you remember the controversy about the SST, a supersonic transport plane designed to operate in the stratosphere? That was a case of an argument where neither side had all the facts. What would be the effect of introducing oxides of nitrogen into the stratosphere? One textbook reaction shows it to reduce the ozone content. Would that change the climate? Would it cause the incidence of skin cancers to increase?

Ozone—a molecule of three oxygen atoms rather than the usual two—is formed in the upper atmosphere under the influence of the ultraviolet rays of the sun. Ozone between 50,000 and 165,000 feet (15–50 km), where it is two hundred times more abundant than near the surface, keeps most of the ultraviolet radiation from reaching the ground. Exposure to ultraviolet rays unquestionably causes skin cancers.

After several years of study the National Academy of Science reported its conclusions in 1975. Some changes in the climate and temperature can be expected when a substantial number of jets fly in the stratosphere. What the changes would be cannot be determined at this time.

Skin cancer would definitely increase. With present ozone levels, 10,000 cases of melanoma and 400,000 cases of less dangerous skin cancers occur in the United States each year. The operation of one hundred planes of the Concorde or Tupelov 144 designs would increase the incidence 1.4 per cent. Result: 140 more melanoma cases each year, 5,600 more of the less dangerous skin cancers.

Larger, higher flying planes similar to the SST would increase the skin-cancer rate 6 per cent for every hundred planes in operation. That is 600 added melanoma cases, 24,000 more of the less serious skin cancers per year in the United States.

Recently another alarm was sounded: The protective ozone was being destroyed by Freon, released by industry, leaking from refrigerators and air-conditioners, and squirted from aerosol cans, where it is used to propel shaving cream, antiperspirants, and insecticides.

Industry spokesmen say that no connection between their product and cancer has been proven. So still do cigarette manufacturers.

The winds that link the world make most of it livable by distributing heat and moisture. And they help thin out the particles and gases man dumps constantly into the atmosphere.

In a different sense of the word the winds have also linked the whole world in unheard-of co-operation between nations.

It started in 1873 with the founding of the World Meteorological Organization. International organizations are common. One, the Postal Union, lets you send letters and parcels to virtually every country in the world.

But weather observations are the most perishable of goods. The observations of seven thousand surface weather stations, thousands of ships—about to be augmented by a global system of ocean buoys—and hundreds of upper-air soundings become known within the hour by teletype, cable, and radio.

An international code has overcome all language problems. The first five figures of any message identify the observing station, whether you call it Wien, Vienna, Vienne, or whatever. The next single figure indicates sky cover. Code 0 means no clouds, 8 a sky completely covered by clouds, whatever the words for cloud and sky in your language. The next two figures give wind direction; 32, for example, means the wind is from 320°, which in English you'd call northwest.

And you can use whatever units you please. The next two figures give the speed of the wind. You can read 20 as 18–22 knots (nautical miles per hour), as 21–25 statute miles per hour, as 9–11 meters per second, or as so many kangaroo hops per minute.

Weather maps of the entire northern hemisphere are automatically drawn, and distributed by facsimile, at the World Meteorological Centers in Washington and Moscow; for the southern hemisphere in Melbourne, Australia.

More than two hundred government stations in one hundred countries directly receive the automatic picture transmission from orbiting satellites; another four hundred such receivers are at universities and at private weather services. The system is so simple that several hundred amateurs have built their own apparatus.

In all sciences the people in the same field follow developments in other countries, exchange data, experimental findings, and theories. But in no other field has there been such joint international research as in meteorology.

And with good reason. We now know that a patch of cool surface water west of Hawaii will influence the weather—even the

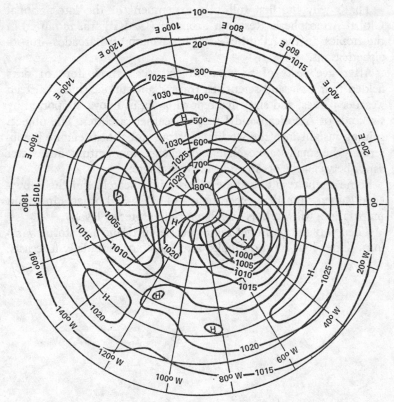

38. Weather map of entire northern hemisphere

year's climate—not only in California but in the *eastern* United States. Or that a rise in sea level on Truk indicates specific weather and current patterns halfway around the world in North and South America. Think about it: The sea level measured there helps predict, for instance, the year's catch of anchovies off Peru more than 6,000 nautical miles (10,000 km) to the east.

That both examples—Hawaii and Truk—refer to the tropics is no accident. In these zones of energy surplus, the weather patterns and climate of the whole world are born. They also happen to be the area of the sparsest weather observations.

That's why the first full-scale experiment of the international Global Atmospheric Research Program (GARP) was mounted in the tropics. In the Atlantic—after a warm-up off Barbados—for logistic reasons.

After five years of preparation sixty-six nations for 101 days fielded four thousand scientists, thirty-eight surface ships, thirteen weather planes, and sixty-five reporting ocean buoys, supported by six kinds of American and Russian weather satellites. The object: gaining insight into the workings of the global heat engine by observing the small-scale exchange of energy, momentum, and water vapor between the ocean and the atmosphere.

Some of the results may be called pure research. But the knowledge gained from that experiment—GATE—and others already in preparation, will work its way down to the forecast level.

Then you and I will get more precise hurricane and storm warnings, better long-term outlooks, and more accurate daily forecasts.

Index

X